A VIEW FROM THE BLUE

POLICING BRADFORD WEST YORKSHIRE IN THE 1980S

Author and Illustrator

Tim Mills

Copyright © 2018 by Tim Mills

All rights reserved. No part of this publication may be reproduced, distributed, or transmitted in any form or by any means, including photocopying, recording, or other electronic or mechanical methods, without the prior written permission of the author.

Foreword

In 1981, aged 21years, I joined the West Yorkshire police. This was a period when Britain would be plagued with some of its worst scenes of football hooliganism, large scale public disorder, race riots and political unrest. Ahead lay an equal measure of happy, sad and often stressful times as I worked the streets of Bradford, a tough multicultural northern city.

Some twenty five years since retiring, whilst taking a trip down memory lane, I found myself jotting down a few of my long held recollections. As the pages of fairly illegible scribble grew, I began to add a number of sketches and low-and-behold, it started to look a bit like a book. With a little help from my friends, here we are.

I have avoided writing my book as a documentary, covering every detail from training school to retirement. Instead, I have presented my book as a collection of stories that I hold dear, which I hope you will find entertaining. Many of the submissions are my personal experiences whilst others, such as the heart-rending Bradford City football stadium fire and the still hotly-debated twelve month long miners strike, have become embedded in modern British history.

I was medically retired in 1991, exactly ten years after my induction. I was released with an exemplary service record having been diagnosed with a nervous breakdown. There may be a contradiction there! So that was that - short and not always sweet; over in the blink of an eye yet at times feeling like an eternity, leaving me with timeless memories.

I hope my book will give you a few chuckles and maybe an odd tear as you join me and turn back the clock to what was a unique era of British policing.

Contents

Chapter 1
Blue Light Blues

Chapter 2
Wrong Place for a Mini Estate

Chapter 3
Night Observations Terror

Chapter 4
Hospital Havoc

Chapter 5
Road Traffic Policing

Chapter 6
Bradford Riots

Chapter 7
Down Town Drop Out

Chapter 8
On the Job Training

Chapter 9

Tipsy Tory

Chapter 10

Valley Parade – The Fire

(Bradford City Football Club)

Chapter 11

Metro Vs Cosworth

Chapter 12

More from the Square

Chapter 13

Crushed Emotions

Chapter 14

By Hukka by Crook

Chapter 15

Ned and the Scrap Yard Tealeaf

Chapter 16

Anonymous Call

Chapter 17

When is a Chair Not a Chair

Chapter 18

Miners Strike 1984-85

Chapter 19

Burgler Billy and the Broken Fag

Chapter 20

Football Crazies

Chapter 21

No Place for a Kid

Chapter 22

Treasure Hunt

Chapter 23

One for my Baby

Chapter 24

Home alone

Chapter 25

CID

(Criminal Investigation Department)

Chapter 26

The Writing on the Wall

1

Blue Light Blues

It was almost 10pm on a cold, wet winters evening and I was starting to think about my first pint when I received a radio message instructing me to perform one last task. I wasn't going to hang about with this one, a report of neighbours playing excessively loud music.

My destination was a top floor flat in one of a group of four tower blocks, collectively known as Newby Square. The towers in question were built a short distance apart from one another, together forming a courtyard square, which could only be entered and exited by vehicle via one location. This lack of access to the area together with the strong anti-police nature of a large number of the residents had given the square a reputation similar to that of a fortress, where the police were most definitely not welcome.

Escalating over the past few months, there had been several serious incidents where police units had been dispatched to the square and, upon entering the courtyard, had been confronted with groups of youths who had targeted the officers and their vehicles with bricks and bottles. As a result of the ongoing situation, a directive had been issued from headquarters that no police vehicles were to be driven onto the complex and officers must enter on foot in pairs.

It must have looked good on paper but not always adhered to as here I was responding to a call 'unaccompanied'. As per instructions, I parked my patrol car on a dimly lit side street several blocks away from the square and hot-footed it through the darkness to the base of Hillfoot Tower, a 16 stories tall block of council flats. Once there I took a deep breath and called the elevator. I stepped back as the doors opened, mindful that this could be a trap. It's all good. The lift was clear apart from the statutory misspelt graffiti and the stench of stale urine. In I hopped and started the painfully slow ascent to the top floor, still conscious that at any level I may have received unwanted company.

No, here I was. I made it to the top. Part one complete. I was immediately deafened by the silence and a short walk to the flat in question revealed the door to be boarded up. This was good and not so good as the flat was clearly unoccupied, which suggested the call was almost certainly a hoax. The question now was: what was the real reason for the caller wanting a police presence? So I found myself on the top floor of the semi-derelict Hillfoot tower block with no back up and next to no radio reception. Someone wanted it this way but why?

Back into the elevator and down I went. If something was going to happen it would likely be on one of sixteen floors separating me from the ground level. I was getting a bit pumped by now and with each passing floor the tension was rising. Wow, there it was: ground floor. The doors separated. This was where we could get it on. "I'm ready guys!", I thought.

Nothing! This was really strange - no welcoming party. That was fine by me. I was out of there. I made my way from the square in double quick time and with no messing, threw open the car door and jumped into the Batmobile and away back to base.

I parked the car in the police yard, completed the logbook and handed it over with the keys at the control room hatch and I was away home. Not quite done! I had barely got my arse in front of the TV when my phone rang. "Tim, it's the night shift controller here. Any idea where the blue light has gone from the top of your patrol car, lad?"

2

Wrong Place for a Mini Estate

West Bowling, Bradford: heavily populated, multicultural estate covering a vast area that included private and council homes with the addition of several industrial parks. This would be my designated patrol area for several years as a Community Constable.

On the majority of my shifts I covered the area on foot, which allowed me a closer, more personal contact with the residents, together with a thorough knowledge of the local characters and general layout of the estate. A typical evening shift would see me wander around the estate ensuring that pubs and clubs were emptied with a minimum of problems and seeing that people were able to make their way home safely. Once the pub revellers had cleared the streets I would continue to walk the area checking on vulnerable properties and buildings.

It was on one such night, whilst I was making my routine checks that I came across a scruffy, old Mini estate car which was parked, unattended, at the end of a dark side street close to a school building. My interest in this car was twofold, partly due to its dishevelled condition but also because I hadn't recalled seeing the vehicle on the estate before. A quick once-over of the car revealed all of the doors were unlocked and there was no tax disc displayed in the windscreen. In addition, the boot of the car and the rear seats were loaded with what appeared to be industrial heating equipment. Not a major crime on the face of it and no real reason to be overly concerned. That is until I made a PNC (Police National Computer) enquiry on the vehicle licence plate. Result! The check came back showing the Mini to be registered as stolen and in addition was flagged that any occupants must be approached with caution.

I took up a position behind a nearby wall where I could observe the vehicle without being seen, whilst a pursuit vehicle was dispatched to my location. This was literally the calm before the storm because the moment that the police car came into view at the far end of the street, two men on foot approached the Mini carrying further items of heating equipment similar to those already inside the car. On seeing the police vehicle speeding towards them, the two suspects threw the items they were carrying into the road and quickly entered the Mini.

I was too far away from the men to tackle either of them and, as the pursuit car stopped to collect me, the suspects took the opportunity to take off in the stolen vehicle. As I jumped into the passenger side of the police car, Sergeant Goody began our pursuit of the suspects. This would be no easy task as the streets in this part of the estate were both short and narrow with little or no lighting, which created a dark warren of twists and turns.

Away they went. The laden Mini swerved left then right before bouncing over a kerb edge and scraping along a road sign. Thank God the residents were tucked up in bed. It was around this time that the passenger chose to leap from the moving vehicle. Was that to improve his chance of escape or the terror of his mate's driving? No time to worry about this fella, our priority was the guy ahead of us, whose reckless driving showed no sign of easing. If anything, he was becoming more desperate!

Sure enough, no-ones luck lasts forever and as the Mini was thrown wildly into yet another side street, the front wing collided with the back end of a parked Land Rover, the impact of which bounced the smaller Mini across the street and into a dry stone wall. The driver's door of the stationary car was now wedged tight against what was left of the wall, I pulled open the passenger door and leapt in.

Smack! I was greeted with straight left jab to the kisser. This was clearly what was meant by "approach this man with caution". I let him have one back. It only seemed fair and we proceeded to exchange a few more blows in the confines of our cramped arena. During the scuffle, a pair of dark blue sleeves brushed across the top of my shoulders from behind and took hold of my opponent's collar. (Yes, he had his collar felt). After a short struggle, Goody and I wrestled the guy out of the Mini and into the cop car. The second man who had earlier jumped from the vehicle, didn't make it very far before he too was picked up by the crew of a back up unit that had arrived on the scene.

It turned out that these two out-of-town chancers had been told about a local primary school undergoing a refit and had rolled up to see what was in it for them. As it turned out they got considerably more than they bargained for as both were already on bail for similar offences, and subsequently the pair received custodial sentences for their troubles.

3

Night Observations Terror

Feeling pretty elevated one Autumn night, I had been detailed to keep observations on a vulnerable grocery store from one of the highest points in Bradford. My vantage point gave me a clear view down into the valley overlooking the isolated premises, which had been the target for a number of break-ins over the past few weeks.

So there I was, back in my civvies, my refuge for the evening being the choice of one of three adjoining public toilet blocks, none of which appeared to have seen a Toilet Duck during the last millennium. The location for these toilets was slightly bemusing as they seemed to be some distance from the nearest population and their lofty position left them vulnerable to the chilling breeze that was gently sweeping across the tops. Still, it was what it was and all things being equal, I should have been in for a reasonably quiet night. My only real requirement was to radio in any suspicious activity regarding the property in question. My two biggest challenges seemed to be keeping warm and occupied, as all I had for company was a couple of chocolate bars and a can of pop. Sadly for me, no such thing as a smart phone packed with games and videos. Not back in the 80s!

The first hour or so between midnight and 1.30am offered little more in the way of entertainment than watching several groups of drunken louts staggering past my temporary shelter. I never really established where they were travelling to or from but it did suggest that the toilets were better placed than I had originally thought. It occurred to me as a number of the drunkards passed by me that I was receiving a number of inquisitive glances. Maybe they knew why I was there, or more likely they were not entirely convinced about a guy on his own hovering around at the entrance to a dingy public loo. There was little I could do about that other than hope none of them returned later to satisfy their curiosity.

It had been quiet for a good while when the dreaded mind games started to kick in. Bored, cold and more bored with just the gentle chill breeze to interrupt my thoughts. What was that? Footsteps on the gravel track heading my way accompanied by voices. I couldn't make out what they were saying but it sounded like two, maybe three men, some ten or fifteen yards away to my right. Their steps were deliberate and intermittent, as though someone was trying not to be heard. Then silence followed by whispering. Shit! Definitely three blokes but why were they creeping along?

Not happy, I took a step back into my cubicle. Best arm myself. Quick rummage in the darkness, what's this? Oh shit! A stinking, moth-eaten toilet brush. Not my first choice for a defensive item but it was all I had. It would have to do.

More rustling. They were close now. My arse was puckered up tight enough to play a rendition of the last waltz on a finely tuned picallo. No time for such niceties now. I took up my position close against the door-frame armed with my makeshift plastic baton.

Okay, bring it on, let's rumble. Here they were. My heart was jumping from my chest. One more step and we would be face to face. I made my move and leapt forward, and there they were, my would-be attackers. For fuck sake! An empty crisp packet. Cheese and onion at that. Tumbling along in the night breeze away into the distance.

4

Hospital Havoc

As coppers, we would often find ourselves in the midst of hospital accident and emergency departments: generally busy and often volatile places. Occasionally we would be there at the request of the staff. At other times we would roll up with a problem we had found all by ourselves. This was one of the latter.

My side kick today was Wobbly Gob or Wobbly for short. He joined up about 12 months after me though we were similar in age. Like me Wobbly wasn't one of the biggest guys on the force but he more than made up for that with his courage and commitment. A popular lad on the team he had earned his nickname due to the speed his mouth moved whenever he was excited. Such as the occasion when he tried to relay the registration number phonetically via his radio to the control room, as a stolen vehicle sped past him. "Vehicle number one two three R-Romeo D-Delta Q-Cucumber"

Wobbly and I had initially responded to a domestic dispute in the salubrious area of East Bierley. Here we received a warm welcome from Nobby, who despite it only being 10am had still managed to track down and consume enough alcohol to render himself a drunken and abusive pleb. A well-built fella, he was aggressive enough to require an alert approach when dealing with him.

Nobby's estranged wife, who had called the incident in, now decided it was a good idea to stand by her front door hurling abuse at her ex. A sport which came with the same level of danger as poking a grizzly bear with a short stick.

After a brief exchange of pleasantries between the pair, Nobby felt the need to let fly with a right hook to the nearest lamppost-a party piece he had repeated a number of times over the years. The loud crack and the grimace which replaced the smile on his face suggested to us that Nobby may well have fractured his hand in the process. Oh great, and just like that we're on our way to the A&E.

The reaction from the staff on our arrival was a little less than ecstatic, though we like to think this was largely down to the bundle of joy we had in tow. Nobby had been handcuffed at the scene, partly for his safety but equally for our own. "They'll need to come off so I can examine him." Was the instruction from the duty doctor. Hmmm at the moment the star of the show was presenting himself as a choir boy who could do no wrong but previous encounters with him told me this calm persona was unlikely to last.

"Come on now, I have a lot of others to see." "Okay Doc, your call," and off came the cuffs. "Right let me take a look at the damage." "No, wait up," slurred Nobby. "I need a piss, real bad."

I could see this hadn't impressed the doctor one bit and decided the quicker we could remove Nobby the better it would be all round. Wobbly took one arm while I took the other and we escorted him to the nearest public toilet, within the hospital.

The pratt had no sooner taken aim when the inner demon returned and without warning he began punching wildly with both his injured and uninjured fists against the large mirror facing back at him. As the mirror shattered, firing shards of glass in every direction, urgent action was required to stop the loony and a size nine boot to the back of his right knee did the job nicely. He instantly crumpled forward cracking his head against the top of the porcelain urinal.

Great! Now the injury count is growing. In addition to the original injury, he now had blood running from both hands and a small cut on his forehead.

The knock to his head at least appeared to have taken the wind from his sails and we were able to muscle him back to the A&E. If our original welcome had been a little frosty, the look on the Doc's face was currently leaving nothing to the imagination.

"What have you done now?" he bellowed out towards Nobby. Well, I think it was towards Nobby, who was now wearing a supercilious grin across his face.

"Show me your hands." Still not up to speed that people were trying to help him, he lunged forward and grabbed a scalpel from the nearby surgical tray and proceeded to wave it in the Doctor's face. Quicker than a wild west gun slinger, Wobbly's truncheon came smashing down across the knife wielding forearm and the blade went crashing to the floor.

"Get that animal out of here, now!" It was something in the tone of the instruction that made me think the Doctor had finally had enough of the uninvited guest. So we made our exit, recuffing Nobby before dragging him through reception and across the carpark to our vehicle.

Safely back at the Bridewell the duty Doctor examined and treated the prisoner for his minor injuries. We then placed Noddy in a cell to sleep off his drunken state.

The following morning, in a much calmer frame of mind, Nobby was charged and bailed with the relevant offences. "See ya soon Nobby."

5

Road Traffic Policing

Going to be honest right from the off, this part of the job never offered much appeal to me. Never the less in an effort to cover all bases here we go.

Advanced Driving School

Looking back, whilst I was never likely to pursue a career in road traffic, the two weeks spent at the training school did offer some valuable lessons and more than a little fun.

The course itself was evenly divided between classroom studies, regarding traffic law and case files, and practical sessions, driving a variety of vehicles both on and off road, under the guidance of a qualified advanced police driving instructor.

The hours spent in the classroom were in the main pretty mind numbing but they did offer up some attention grabbing moments. These included the photographs and slide shows of fatal accident scenes such as the family of five who's saloon car was demolished by an articulated wagon, sending the occupants flying to their deaths along a 100 yard stretch of motorway. Ironically the family members came to rest in descending age order. Dad furthest from the wrecked vehicle closely followed by mum, then two toddlers and finally the baby still strapped into her child safety seat. Then there was the middle aged motorcyclist who was taking advantage of the summer sunshine to give his bike a run through the country lanes. He turned a blind bend directly into the path of an oncoming tractor, his neck collided with the bottom edge of the raised digger bucket severing his head.

All these graphic displays were intended to prepare us for the scenes we would likely encounter at some point during our forthcoming careers.

On occasion the classroom would be moved outside to a disused parade ground where we would recreate the scene of a road traffic accident using scrap vehicles and life sized dummies on previously marked out roads. We would split into two teams and alternate between traffic management and tending the victims. The traffic management team would be responsible for making the area safe, using traffic cones to cordon of the vehicles etc, then recording information of the accident such as vehicle and occupants details, road measurements, weather conditions and such like. Whilst team one was busying away the second team would attend to the victims, some of which were dummies whilst others were instructors acting out a part. Some might say it was difficult to tell one from another. The scenarios were brought to life with attendance of the fire service and medical experts.

The advanced driving side of the course was predominately practical and kicked off with the infamous skid pan. Essentially this was a circle of tarmac a little smaller than a football pitch, completely coated in old engine oil and diesel. The whole area was doused in water from a high tech sprinkler system in the form of a lengthy hose pipe, periodically punctured with hundreds of tiny holes, which ran around the perimeter of the tarmac. The combination of the oil and water ensured the whole of the surface was more slippery than a well polished ice rink, before we took turns driving onto the man made slick in a beat up old Ford Escort fitted with tyres devoid of any visible tread. This exercise was hilarious as we attempted to manoeuvrer the motorized ice skate around a series of cunningly placed plastic traffic cones. The instructors allowed us plenty of time alone on the rink until we started to get a bit cocky at which point they would set two of us loose in two separate vehicles. Starting at opposite ends of a figure of eight layout our only instructions were to completed two laps of the circuit in the quickest time possible without touching any of the cones and most importantly avoiding each others vehicles. Not surprisingly this proved much easier said than done and by the end of the day the vehicles were retired with steam and smoke billowing out from beneath the bonnet and the majority of body panels damaged from repeated collisions. All the fun aside some valuable and lasting driving skills were acquired. The use of anti-lock steering, simply put its the technique of turning the front wheels into a slide, such as when the back end of the car looses traction with the road surface and slides out to the left or right. Turning the front wheels in the same direction as the back end is sliding, together with increasing or reducing the power (These were all rear wheel drive cars) effectively creates a controlled drift, at least that's the intended result. A more useful technique I acquired was 'Cadence braking'. This is particularly useful when driving in wet or icy conditions, when traditional heavy braking simply causes the tyres to lose grip and the vehicle to slide forwards. Cadence braking is the use of intermittent pressure on the brake pedal, essentially a dabbing on and off the pedal which prevents the wheels from locking and sliding out of control. Whatever you do DO NOT take my advice or explanation as to how or when to use these techniques, book yourself an advanced driving lesson with an approved instructor and reap the rewards.

Much less fun were the many hours we spent sat alongside one of the instructors driving around the roads close to the driving centre. The object of this exercise was to improve the scholars awareness of day to day traffic situations improving observational skills and reactions. There was nothing particularly earth shattering, just good old common sense and reading the road ahead. It is impossible to cover even a fraction of the thousands of possible hazards in the space of two weeks, but these are a few of the examples we touched on. Someone running out from behind a parked car into the road, the same parked car pulling into your path without warning. A vehicle entering your carriageway from a side junction, the zebra crossing ahead, someone appears from no where and starts to run across it. The possibilities are endless but the message was, and is simple, expect the unexpected and give yourself extra time to react.

As the course came to a close, we had one treat left, piloting the fully tuned 2.3 litre RS Cosworth. A one of blast through the Yorkshire countryside. We were split into groups of three and assigned an instructor. Initially we were each given thirty minutes driving around a disused airfield getting a feel for the power and handling characteristics, both of which were vastly different from the relatively feeble patrol cars we had meandered round in previously. Test runs out of the way we headed off to the narrow, winding and undulating outback. The rookie trio received one last team briefing regarding the ever changing road surfaces and blind bends which lay ahead, before I took charge of the beast. My final instruction was to drive as fast as possible, ignoring trivialities such as speed restrictions. Enough said, I'd raced motocross bikes for years, that was music to my ears. A handful of revs, clutch out and I was away with a lovely screeching wheel spin. Up a slight incline, round a sharp left bend, followed by a sweeping right-hander and still climbing. Another right then a horseshoe left, straighten up and foot down over a hump leaving the ground for a second or two. "Faster Millsy. You said you were a racer." The Instructor shouted in my ear. Now I have to admit that stung my pride, I thought I was giving this motor a real good thrashing. Still more he wanted, more he would get. "Right Mills floor it. This is a nice straight section." I didn't require a second invitation my right boot was pushing down on the accelerator for all I was worth. There was hardly time to take my eyes from the road ahead but a brief glance at the speedo told me we had topped the ton. Breaching the 100mph was pretty exhilarating on a road which was covered in gravel, leaves and the occasional dollop of sheep shit, and was little more than a couple of foot wider than the car. Then. Out of the blue, well the trees on my left to be exact, a short distance ahead, a pheasant decided to jump out of a heavily wooded area and make its way across the road to the trees on the opposite side. I had a flash back, what was it they told us last week about expecting the unexpected and reaction time, what a load of bollocks that seemed right now. My decision making time was down to a nano second, infact it was down to pure instinct. Its fair to say pheasants can run at a reasonable pace, especially with a tonne of speeding metal bearing down on them, that said road runner himself wouldn't have been quick enough to reach safety in this situation. My mind was set. No way was I going to run over this little fella. I scrubbed off as much speed as I could then threw the car onto the grass verge between the edge of the road and the line of trees. This was a risk for sure. No shit. Having two wheels on the solid tarmac and two on the grassy bank was at best unpredictable. But I did it. I will concede it was more by luck than judgement, but hey the pheasant survived and the car and its occupants were fine. Well physically at least. "Stop the car Mills. Now you twat!" It seemed the instructor was regretting his earlier request for more speed. A few yards on I brought the car to a halt. "Right out. Everybody get out." Wow the instructor really wasn't in a good place. "Mills you fucking wanker. What the fuck were you thinking? You could have fucking killed us all." He seemed a little stressed. Not sure if this was all part of the assessment. I had to respond with something. "That's true. But I didn't, and the bird made it as well." I'm pretty sure this didn't help. "Right everybody back in the fucking car." Before I could take a step forward the instructor issued a more specific directive. "Not the fucking drivers seat Mills. Dont you go near that. Get in the fucking back. I don't want to see you again. Ever." He really hadn't taken my evasive action very well at all. I considered asking him if he was in the right frame of mind to drive, but thought better of it.

The following day we received our final marks regarding suitability for a future position within the rapid response team. I didn't make the grade. Oh well horses for courses.

So, just like that my advanced driver training was over.

Sub-Divisional Traffic Attachment

I'm sure it wont come a major surprise when I tell you that the majority of a traffic cops shift is divided between all manor of routine motoring incidents, examining vehicles for defects, recording driver details and their documents, organising and implementing speed traps, inspecting and weighing heavy goods vehicles, traffic management and monitoring, vehicle escort duties etc. Please stop I hear you say. Fair enough, but to redress the balance, the remainder of the traffic cops time would often involve high speed car chases, dealing with serious road accidents, drink driving (Not the officers. Of course) and rapid response to major incidents.

And so I began my two week secondment alongside road traffic officer Sergeant Brown.

Sergeant Brown was a nice guy, very quiet, in his late forties, married, though he never talked about his wife. He was balding and massively over weight but fiercely proud of his twenty years road traffic experience.

We were about to spend the next fourteen shifts within the confines of a Rover 3.5 litre SDI rapid response car. Not an all together thrilling prospect. I loved sport. He didn't. He was a railway enthusiast. I wasn't. Still I was there to learn the ropes of traffic policing, and he was the guy to deliver, so an open mind was required.

The first few days did little to enhance my pre-conceived ides of the road traffic fraternity, repeatedly pulling over vehicles for minor infringements such as a light out, dirty number plates, ugly driver, pretty much any excuse to stop a vehicle. These stop and checks would often reveal further offences such as bald tyres, defective indicators, no vehicle tax or failing to display a tax disc (No longer required with the advent of the internet). A check on the police national computer (PNC) would reveal the owners name and address, whether or not the vehicle was stolen, and additional information such as the vehicle was used by a known criminal or a disqualified driver. If everything appeared to be on the level a form HORT 1 (No idea what that stands for) or a producer, as they were more commonly called, would be issued to the driver who would have seven days to attend a designated police station to produce the relevant driving documents. The vehicle checks occasionally bore fruit in unexpected ways, revealing drugs, weapons, stolen goods amongst other things.

One copper experienced just such a career high, or is that a low, whilst making a routine check when he pulled over a vehicle with a tail light out in the Manningham area of Bradford. He approached the driver of the car explaining to him why he had been stopped, to which the driver suggested he took a look inside the boot of the car. He did, and much to his amazement he discovered the body of a young woman who had earlier been strangled by the driver.

It remained a valuable lesson. You never could predict what a simple vehicle check might reveal.

Aside from the numerous vehicle checks, speed monitoring exercises, and directing traffic at faulty traffic lights etc my first response to a serious incident came via a message from the control room instructing us to attend a road traffic accident, where a young boy had been knocked off his bicycle at Laisterdyke traffic lights. We responded at speed, Browny flicked on the bells, whistles, lights and sirens and we were on our way. I have to give credit where its due, even at high speed Sgt Browns driving style made me feel relaxed and confident, something that can't be said of a good many of my colleagues. So this was my first real call to action and my adrenalin was pumping. We reached the scene in minutes to find traffic already building up on both sides of the traffic lights. A small group of people had gathered around a Ford Cortina, which had both front doors open and was stationary at the corner of the lights. Sgt Brown parked our vehicle behind the Cortina, effectively shielding it from oncoming traffic. As I stepped out of the police car I could see a twisted pedal cycle laid in the centre of the road some two or three yards infront of the Cortina. Along with Sgt Brown I approached the open drivers door only to find the vehicle empty. However directly below me was a young lad laying on his back with just his head visible from beneath the car. The lad looked scared, but smiled and in a breathless voice apologised for causing us problems, as I knelt beside him. Above me I was aware the Sgt Brown had located the driver of the Cortina who was explaining how the boy had ridden his bike off the pavement directly infront of his car giving him no time to avoid a collision. Oh if only he'd been on my awareness course. Whilst they were talking I laid on the road and peered underneath the car. The situation didn't look to comfortable for my young friend, despite there being no obvious signs of heavy bleeding, his legs were bent at very unnatural angles to his body which appeared to be pinned to the road by the underside of the Cortina. I established the boy was fourteen and his name was John. "Okay John, you're doing great. Try and keep still and we'll have you out in no time. How are you feeling?" "I'm okay sir, but I can't feel my legs." Now my medical knowledge is limited at best, but that didn't sound good. I took my jacket off and placed it over Johns chest. His head felt cool and clammy. I spoke to Sgt Brown and updated him on Johns condition. He told me to keep talking to John but under no circumstances was I to move him, the ambulance was on its way. I had no sooner returned to John when I heard the sirens of the ambulance as it approached. "Not long now John the ambulance is here." I reassured him. "How you doing pal?" Johns smile had disappeared. "I'm scared." He said. I stepped to the side for the ambulance crew. "You'll be fine John, let these people take a look at you. I'll be right here." The truth was I couldn't let Johns condition distract me, there was still work to be done. I took out my note book and made my way over to the crowd of people in search of witnesses. As I looked around I could see there were at least three other police cars in attendance and uniformed officers were directing traffic through the lights and around the Cortina which had been cordoned off. A loud siren heralded the arrival of the fire brigade. Having obtained the details from a handful of witnesses I rejoined Sgt Brown. We too were spectators now, as the fire officers, with the aid of their hydraulic lifting equipment, slowly raised the Cortina clear of John, sufficiently for the ambulance crew to move in, which they did, quickly. I was aware the medics main concerns were spinal injuries and internal bleeding, and that swift conveyance to the hospital had to be balanced with extreme caution whilst moving the injured party. I believed John was in good hands, and all I could do now was hope. As the ambulance left the scene and made its way to the hospital the crowd of onlookers began to drift away, leaving me and Browny to conclude our examination. We obtained measurements and made sketches of the positions of the Cortina and the crumpled bike, before both were removed to the police compound to be checked over by the vehicle examination team for possible defects. Having finished at the scene we made our way to the hospital for an update on Johns condition. The news was in the main great, no internal bleeding, and no spinal or organ damage. However it would be months of rehabilitation and several operations on his legs before John was able to walk again. In order to complete our enquiries Sgt Brown and I, well mainly me, had to obtain a number of written statements from witnesses, before compiling a full accident report file for the consideration of the Crown Prosecution Services, who in turn concluded no charges were to be brought against any of the parties involved.

Upside Down Car

Not all the incidents I attended were the result of information supplied by the public via my control room, on occasion a situation would just present itself out of the blue. One of these random encounters occurred as myself and Browny were driving back to Bradford one evening around 10pm, having obtained a couple of witness statements in Heckmondwike. As we approached the Red Pelican restaurant situated on the A638 some 17 miles outside of Bradford our conversation was silenced as we gazed at the most surreal sight which appeared before us.

A BMW saloon car had come to a halt, effectively upside down, at a 45 degree angle to the road surface, its wheels exposed to the night sky, and smoke billowing out from beneath the bonnet which was wedged against the perimeter wall, close to an archway which lead to the restaurant entrance The most likely explanation for the positioning of the car seemed to be the that driver had completely misjudged his entry into the archway, clipped a curb and flipped the car over.

Yet there were no other vehicles and no onlookers. It had to have happened literally seconds before we arrived.

Myself and Browny ran to the stricken vehicle fully expecting to find people trapped inside. The drivers door was partially open and the ceiling light illuminated the interior. No one there. The car was empty. "Quick" Shouted Sgt Brown "Look under the car. The driver can't be far away." I grabbed a torch from the back of the traffic car and hurried back to the scene. I shone the beam of light under the wreck. Nothing. Whoever had been driving the BMW had vanished. The windscreen though shattered had remained in place, suggesting the driver may have been thrown through the open door on impact. A search of the grounds revealed nothing, and no one inside the restaurant was even aware of the accident. We returned to the BMW and requested back up units, our concern for the driver and anyone else who may have been in the car were growing. Whilst it appeared the occupants had survived the initial impact, it was more than likely there would be injuries, quite likely serious injuries. "Maybe if he's in shock he could have made his way along the road side." I offered. "Fair shout" replied Sgt Brown "But if so which way?" Our predicament was halved as the first back up units arrived. They set off in one direction we took the other. Half a mile along the road, nothing. A quick radio call to the other lads revealed they too had drawn a blank. With time and ideas running short I suggested we leave the road and make our way through the trees into the field beyond. Without so much as a nod Browny was already pushing his way through the thicket. We elected to walk round the perimeter of the field, which proved to be no picnic as the 3 acre field had been recently ploughed and was waterlogged from earlier rainfall. So we pushed on desperate to find someone from the wreckage. I followed behind Browny as he alternated the beam of torch light from the trees to the centre of the field and back again. Then in a eureka moment I saw a face staring back at me from within the trees. "He's here Sarge, this way." I shouted as I ran, well dragged my feet through the clinging mud, until I reached a man in his early twenties, who was crouching under some branches. "You okay pal." I asked him. "Yeah I'm fine. Where's my girlfriend?" Oh shit this was not what we wanted to hear. "There is no one else in the car, are you sure she was with you?" I asked thinking he may be concussed. I'm pretty sure." He slurred. "I was with her earlier. I think." The slur in his words and the stench of alcohol on his breath offered up a likely explanation for the cause of the accident. He was drunk. "Right I need you to be very clear. Was anyone with you in the car?" "Err, no, no now I think about it I left her at her flat." At which he began to laugh to himself. After satisfying ourselves that he was okay to be moved we escorted him to the traffic car where I administered my first breathalyser test. Bingo. Instant red light, he had proved positive and I arrested him for drink driving. Back at the nick he was examined by a doctor and given a night in the cells to sleep off the alcohol. The following morning during an interview with myself and Sgt Brown he admitted to driving whilst over the limit, claiming the 10 pints of lager had caused him to fall asleep at the wheel, after which he remembered nothing until I found him.

He subsequently lost his driving licence and paid out a few quid in fines. The fact that no one else was injured and he himself suffered nothing more than a few cuts and bruises defied logic.

If there can be a winner in these circumstances, then he was surely it.

Motorcycle Scapegoat

One week into my traffic secondment I was approached by Sgt Brown "You're the motorcycle enthusiast." He declared and handed me a road traffic accident report. "Young knob head biker. He's bang to rights, nearly killed a little kid. Just get a few statements and lets get him to court." I was a little surprised at Browny's cut and dried opinions, but if it was down to me to investigate the accident I was going to do it without any pre conceived ideas.

The report outlined a serious accident which had occurred the previous afternoon in a residential area, when a motorcycle had collided with an eight year old boy. The result of the collision had left the boy with serious head injuries in a coma, being treated in the intensive care unit at the Bradford Royal Infirmary. Following the accident the boys family had made allegations that the rider of the motorcycle, a seventeen year old lad, regularly road his motor bike up and down their street at speed, often pulling wheelies and generally being reckless. They claimed that whilst they had not witnessed the accident take place, this would almost certainly be the reason for their sons injuries. To add more pressure to the enquiry the local paper had got hold of the story and they too had been quick to lay full blame at the hands of the biker. Looking back it would have been much easier to go with the masses and appease the over riding opinion and just nail the biker to the cross but that was something I wasn't prepared to do. Any thoughts I might have had about ducking out of the challenge were quickly quashed by Sgt Brown. "Okay Millsy get yourself to the scene, liaise with me with anything and everything you find. I'm off to the hospital to see how the young boy is doing." And just like that, I was officer in charge of what felt like a major incident. I drove to the street where the accident had occurred and found myself at the entrance to a nice clean, well kept cul-de-sac lined on both sides with privately owned semi-detached houses. I noted that at the foot of the cul-de-sac a dirt track led to an open area of grassy waste land. There were lines of cars parked on both sides of the street and I was drawn to the large number of kids playing on the pavements outside the houses. There must have been a dozen or more ranging from 5 to 10 years of age. Armed with my note pad I took a deep breath and knocked on the door of the injured boys house. The door was opened and a man in his early thirties stood before me. The man introduced himself as Mr Evans and confirmed that he was the father of the injured boy, Jamie. I listened as he reiterated the allegations regarding the motorcyclist's previous dangerous riding, but he concluded that he had not seen anything on the afternoon in question, until one of the children who had been playing in the street called at this house with the bad news.

I retuned to my car to gather my thoughts, Mr Evans was understandably angry, why wouldn't he be? If it was my boy I would want someone to be made responsible, to pay the price. There was little doubt in my mind that the biker probably had done some stupid stunts previously, so I could justify charging him for this incident whether it was his fault or not. No. I couldn't. I had to obtain unbiased and honest witness accounts and compile a report which reflected the facts. That would prove to be easier said than done as the witnesses were all young children who had heard their parents opinions as to what may or may not have happened.

I returned to the station and spoke with Sgt Brown. News from the hospital was that Jamie was still in a coma and the next few days would be crucial.

The report from the officer s who had first attended the scene suggested that the injuries to Jamie had occurred when one of the wing mirrors mounted on the handle bars of the motorcycle had collided with the side of his head. Details of the motorcycle and the rider had been recorded in the report. The motorcycle a 50cc trail style machine had been seized and impounded, and following an examination blood and hairs were found on the back of the left side mirror, the glass from which had been shattered, all of which was consistent with Jamie's injuries.

At the home of the motorcyclist in company with Sgt Brown I spoke with the seventeen year old owner of the bike who introduced himself as Rick. In the presence of his father Rick was cautioned and an interview took place. Throughout the interview Ricks answers remained consistent, openly admitting that he regularly rode down the cul-de-sac in order to ride on the grass land at the far end even volunteering that he had on occasions pulled wheelies, accepting now, how stupid and dangerous that was. Significantly, though not surprisingly, his account of how the accident occurred differed greatly from the original allegations forwarded by Jamie's family. He remained adamant that on the day in question he had done nothing to cause the accident. "I swear on that day I wasn't doing anything stupid, I wasn't even riding fast. As I approached the field at the end of the cul-de-sac the young boy just ran out in front of me from behind a parked car, I tried to swerve away from him, but I had no chance." More questions were asked and answered before I concluded the interview explaining to Rick that I may need to speak to him again.

At this stage I had the details of the motorcyclist and the injured boy, and a statement from the rider outlining his version of events. What I needed now was reliable independent witnesses.

Two days since the accident and I was back on duty, Jamie was out of his coma. It seemed that everyone locally was aware of the accident and opinions were becoming more vocal.

I grabbed my statement forms and headed to the cul-de-sac. It seemed logical to speak to the girl who had been chasing Jamie and had subsequently alerted his dad. As I strode towards the girls house, confirmation of local feelings surfaced when a guy walking his dog shouted towards me "Have you charged the little shit head that nearly killed Jamie yet?" He didn't wait for an answer. At the house the young girls dad ushered me inside. As would be the case with all my witnesses due to them being under the age of 16 they had to be accompanied by a parent. This particular girl was called Clare, she was aged 10 and turned out to be an extremely solid witness. She told me how she had seen the biker many times riding along the cul-de-sac and how he occasionally did wheelies explaining to me what she understood that to mean. Though she did not know the rider by name she was aware of the colour scheme of his machine and its distinctive sound which she said was louder than any of his friends bikes. With regard to the afternoon in question she explained that just prior to the accident she had been chasing Jamie along the pavement in a game of touch and run. She had been unaware of the motorcycle approaching when Jamie ran from the pavement between two parked cars and into the road. She saw the motorcycle collide with Jamie knocking him to the ground at which point she ran straight to Jamie's house to tell his mum and dad. During the statement Clare's dad interrupted his daughter a number of times asking her to reconsider her opinion as to whether the bike was speeding or doing wheelies. "Don't be scared Clare no one will hurt you." He assured her. "No dad." She snapped back at him. "I'm not scared and no he wasn't going fast. I know because the engine sounds louder when he does."The next few weeks were filled visiting and interviewing almost a dozen youngsters who's names were given to me by Clare. The majority of their statements were effectively useless with the exception of one obtained from a young boy similar in age to Jamie. He stated he was on the opposite side of the road to Clare and saw the motorcycle being ridden towards the grass land when he saw Jamie run out infront of the bike. He further corroborated Clare by saying he to believed the motorcycle was not being ridden fast and nor was it doing wheelies.

I had spent weeks speaking to kids, obtaining statements, and trying to get to the truth and in my mind I had. Like it or not, and there were lots who didn't. Still the final decision was not mine to make and detailed court papers were compiled and submitted to the Crown Prosecution Service for their consideration.

During this time Jamie had made great progress and he was expected to make a full recovery though it would be several months before he was back to his normal self.

Some three months after the CPS made their decision not to pursue any charges against Rick I was on foot patrol when by chance I met Jamie's dad. Any lingering doubts about how I had dealt with this incident were completely dispelled when Mr Evans shook my hand and thanked me for the professional and thorough way I had gone about establishing the facts. He went on to say that he had finally got his son home and he was doing really well. As a result friends and family were having a celebratory get together the following weekend and he would be pleased if I could attend.

Know When To Shut Up

Whilst travelling along the busy Wakefield Road dual carriageway, a motorcyclist took it upon himself to overtake our marked police car which was travelling at the 40mph speed limit. Sgt Brown who was not a bloke to lose his cool shouted out. "Look at that wanker, what must the other road users think. He's left me no choice I'll have to pull him." A few yards further along the road Browny flicked on the siren and signalled to the biker to pull over to the side of the road. A few gestures of displeasure were displayed by the bike rider before he reluctantly brought his machine to a halt. "Right Millsy point out this idiots mistake and don't take any shit." I approached the rider a bloke in his late twenties who had already removed his helmet. Before I could utter a word he started. "Oh here we go typical coppers, persecuting the innocent bikers." Again I attempted to speak, but he clearly had more to say. "All these cars flying up and down but oh no it has to be the guy on a bike that gets pulled everytime. Its victimization that's what this is. Why don't you go catch a burglar or something?" And so he continued for several minutes digging his hole deeper and deeper. "Okay that's great have you finished now?" I seized my moment as he paused for breath. "First of all I'm a biker myself, have been since I was a kid. Secondly what exactly did you think would happen when you blast past a brightly marked cop car, which is already at the speed limit. Is this your bike?" His response suggested he just wasn't getting the message. "Course it is you muppet. Do you think I would overtake a cop car on a nicked bike." Now it was my turn to enjoy myself. "Are you in a hurry to get somewhere?" I asked him. "Yes I am as it happens." He snapped. "Oh good this might take some time." If he hadn't been a silly boy and just eaten a bit of humble pie he'd have been on his way. As it was he had failed the attitude test and now it was my turn. The next twenty minutes must have felt like an eternity for him as I recorded his and the bikes details, made countless checks via the police computer, examined every part of his bike, nuts, bolts, lights, brakes, tyres eveything. In the end there wasn't anything substantial to take him to court with, but I'd had a bit of fun and maybe, just maybe he'd learned a life lesson. Reap what you sow.

Drink Yourself to Death

It was about one thirty in the morning when Browny and me got a call to attend a report of a car crashing into a stone wall. The accident had occurred on an isolated country lane just outside our boundary area but we were the nearest quick response vehicle, so sirens and strobe lights on and away we went. It took less than 10 minutes to arrive at the scene and sure enough there was a Datsun saloon car with its front end crumpled into a dry stone wall. The caller for reasons best known to themselves hadn't waited to talk to us. The only occupant inside the car was an Asian male in his mid forties who was pinned into the drivers seat by the steering wheel. He was conscious, but that was pretty much the only positive news. He had blood running from his nose, mouth and ears and he didn't appear aware that we were present. I don't know if it was shock or fear perhaps both, but I can still recall the look of terror etched across his face as I approached the passenger side of the car. The drivers door was wedged up against what remained of the wall and access through the passenger side was also blocked due to the impact buckling the body work, preventing the door from opening. As I peered into the car through the passenger window I was able to see that the drivers lower legs were trapped beneath the rear of the engine which had been pushed backwards through the bulkhead. It was clear this guy was in serious trouble and required urgent medical attention. Ambulance and fire brigade units had been requested and were on route. The accident location was fairly remote and I couldn't be sure how long the back up teams would be, and this fella needed help now, even if it was nothing more than words of reassurance. Due to the twisted nature of the cars body work the normal entry points into the car had been sealed shut and the only thing I could do now was smash the back window and crawl inside. Once inside I leant forward to talk to the injured guy and I was immediately overwhelmed by the stench of stale alcohol. I noticed his breathing was very shallow and laboured as I tried to offer a few words of comfort whilst his wide eyes remained transfixed on the shattered windscreen. He seemed to be trying to respond to me but his words were incoherent and garbled masked by the bloody bubbles which flowed from his mouth. I checked him for any injuries that I might be able to treat, but the cuts to his face and hands appeared superficial compared to his crumpled legs and internal injuries which he had almost certainly sustained. I felt completely useless this guy was dying at the side of me and there was nothing I could do. Flashing blue lights, in an otherwise unlit road, heralded the arrival of the ambulance and fire brigade, which offered fresh optimism. My job was done for now, and I exchanged places with a paramedic via the rear window.

Together with Sgt Brown I watched on as the respective experts played their parts.

An oxygen mask was placed on the injured guy, whilst information was passed between the paramedic and his colleagues and before long it was the turn of the fire fighters who used their hydraulic cutting equipment to remove the roof from the mangled Datsun. Portable floodlights had been erected to illuminate the scene, displaying the full extent of the carnage, against the cold back drop of the dark surroundings.

Even for a layman the enormous difficulty in removing the injured party from the wreckage was obvious, yet there was no option and work began on lifting the engine from his shattered legs. It seemed to take an eternity before he was hoisted from what remained of the car still strapped to the drivers seat.

As the injured man was placed into the ambulance a harrowing silence descended, as despite the best efforts of those involved the driver of the car had died.

Van to Van

What should have been a steady, early evening midweek shift was about to take a twist.

I was accompanying Andy in the Ford Transit divisional van, on route to return a number of recovered stolen items back to their rightful owners.

Andy was a big lad in his early thirties with a good few years service under his belt. He seemed to know the job inside out and was content to remain as a uniform cop with no desire to work his way up the ladder.

Our destination was an address in Horsforth a few miles outside our sub-divisional boundary. As we travelled along Harrogate road a scruffy yellow Transit van pulled out in front of us from a side junction, causing Andy to dab the brakes and scrub off some speed. I didn't think it was such a big deal, but Andy's face was a picture. He was not a happy bunny. "The wanker. I'm pulling him over." Yeah go for it." I encouraged him. "I'll run a check on the plates." It was at that moment that things started to look a little less straight forward. As I peered at the number plate attached to the rear of the van ahead, I found myself reciting the digits of an Irish registration. Now I may well have leapt to a stereotypical conclusion in an instant, but it could hardly have been anything else. Irish number plates on a scruffy tranny van being driven with no regard to other road users. Travellers. Bradford and surrounding areas have always been inundated with large numbers of travellers some good some not so good.

We continued to follow the van whilst waiting for a reply from our vehicle check request. We waited and we waited and still we waited. "Wankers! That's it I'm not waiting any longer. I'm pulling em." Right on cue the radio crackled. "Your vehicle check isn't coming back with a match of any kind. It might be worth stopping the vehicle and see what the occupants have to say." No shit. Why didn't we think of that? "Right Millsy. Flick the blue light on." I duly obliged with Andy's request and the blue roof light started to flash. Now for most people this would be a hint to pull over to the side of the road. Not so for the occupants of our Irish van, nope they saw it as a signal to accelerate away from us. Andy was in no mood to let this one get away, and responded by putting his foot down. A few yards ahead I could see several cars backed up at a red traffic signal. This should have brought the chase to an early conclusion. But no. Instead of coming to a halt behind the stationary vehicles the yellow van swung out to the right into the oncoming lane. Absolute madness, by shear luck there was no traffic approaching us and the tranny van sped through the red lights on the wrong side of the road at a good 60mph. Lady luck played her part again as there were no vehicles in the middle of the junction or entering the junction from either side. Just as well as the driver of the Irish van appeared to have no plans on stopping. Andy was in the zone now, muttering to himself as he clung to the tail of the van ahead. The driver of the van was becoming increasingly reckless and needed to be brought to a stopped before someone got hurt. As it happened we didn't have to wait much longer because less than a mile further on, the road narrowed. It was still one lane in each direction, with a pathway at either side which were lined with solid Yorkshire stone walls. We still needed a bit of divine intervention, which came in the form of a bin wagon. Its reasonable to say the refuge boys aren't always the most considerate lads to other road users, and fortunately for us today was no different. Whether or not the wagon driver had seen the commotion approaching him in his wing mirrors he conveniently, for us, brought his truck to an abrupt halt smack in the middle of the road, effectively preventing the yellow van from passing on either side. Smoke billowed from the yellow vans tyres as the driver slammed on his brakes bringing the van to a halt touching the rear of the bin wagon. Andy seized the moment and quickly brought the police van to a stop tight against the rear bumper of the stranded Irish van, ensuring it couldn't be reversed out. Myself and Andy sprinted to the front of the yellow van expecting the driver to do a runner. Instead, a white guy in his early 30's, with greasy blonde hair, a dirty white tee shirt and torn jeans, casually stepped from his van onto the pavement. The words "What the fuck were you thinking?" Had hardly left my lips when we found ourselves surrounded by five men aged between 20 and 40 all in similar attire to the van driver, who I guessed must have joined us from the rear of the van via the sliding side door. The oldest of the five who happened to be the largest, and sported a large nose which sat at 90 degrees to his face, shouted an instruction to the driver which went something like, "Dant ya be a tellin em anyting ya ear ma?"

It was a strange language, like a mixture between Irish and Alien. Anyone who has watched the film 'Snatch' where Brad Pitt plays the part of a Gipsy bare knuckle fighter, will know exactly what I'm trying to replicate.

The driver responded to his clan members instruction by saying "Naa, I is saying nutten to dese ear fuckers." which he completed with a large smug grin on his face. "What's your name and address laughing boy?" "I aint ta tell ya what is I dan and I dan ave na name for ya." What little I could comprehend from his reply made little or no sense, but it was good enough to take as a refusal to provide details. "Ya boy fuckin nutten an ya right there boy am tell ya keep ya mowt shut." Was the advice offered by his pals. As more officers arrived we took the opportunity to arrest our guy and take him to the nick to establish who the van belonged to.

If we thought things would get any easier back at the nick we were wrong!

Prior to the interview with our man he requested a solicitor. The duty solicitor was contacted and Mr Davies attended.

Duty solicitors were on call to assist those who were unable to provide their own representation.

Over time I had conducted may interviews across the table with many different solicitors some of whom were sticklers for the rules, where as others were more flexible and seemed to devote more time to those they saw as deserved cases. I think its fair to say Mr d

Davies fit the later category. Having spoken to his client, Mr Davies approached myself and Andy and said. "I can't understand a word the guy is saying. May I suggest we just as the necessary questions and I'll be on my way." It was agreed this seemed the best way forward.

At the time of the arrest a request was sent to the police in Ireland to try and locate the last known owner of the van and establish its current status. This was a long shot which was likely to take weeks to resolve, but it would hopefully shed some light on why it was being driven around in West Yorkshire.

The interview commenced with the usual line of questioning. Name, address, date of birth, etc. The prisoners replies seemed to vary, I'm sure his name changed two or three times, but it was difficult to say. As for his address, he was reluctant to commit himself but eventually offered details of a caravan located on an official council approved travellers site.

As the interview continued the address was visited by other officers who informed us thee occupants had unconvincingly confirmed his residence there.

With regard to ownership of the van his answers were at best vague and in the main incoherent, and always followed by a large grin. Mr Davies seemed unable to assist with this line of questioning, looking across at us with a blank expression accompanied with a shrug of his shoulders.

It was becoming clear that my mate Andy had opened a whole can of worms.

Whether it was lucky or not, I'm unsure, but within three hours of the initial arrest the Irish police had traced the current owner of the van who informed them that his nephew had his permission to use it.

With theft of the vehicle no longer on the table, we had only minor driving offences to throw at our boy. A quick chat with the brief and it was agreed that we bail laughing boy to appear at magistrates court at an arranged date to answer several offences including dangerous driving.

As we feared the court hearing was a no show. The occupants from the travellers site had disappeared without a trace, as had the Uncle in Ireland.

An arrest warrant was subsequently issued for our man, which I imagine is still in existence to this day.

The end result for this outing was one to the travellers nil to the coppers, well we still had the van for what that was worth.

It just went to prove you can't win them all.

6

Bradford Riots

The 1980s would prove to be one of the most violent decades in modern British history. It was the height of football gangs and hooliganism, race riots and industrial unrest.

During the summer of 1981, fresh out of training school, I was about to be thrown in at the deep end.

One afternoon whilst out on routine patrol, four of our five units including mine, were called back to the station for a briefing. This was by no means the norm and something pretty big had to be taking place.

On entering the station my thoughts were confirmed. The atmosphere was electric with admin staff running in all directions. An impromptu briefing was held and we were informed by our station Superintendent that large numbers of people, were gathering in the town centre in a demonstration against the earlier arrest of a number of members from the Asian community. Those arrested were being held at the Bradford town centre Bridewell, the centrally based police cells, and the rapidly growing crowd were growing more aggressive as they demanded the release of the prisoners.

I and six other officers were dispatched to Bradford HQ adjacent to the Bridewell, leaving two WPCs to cover the entire Sub Division of Dudley Hill. On arrival at the Bradford HQ we received a further briefing from the Commanding Officer Chief Superintendent Dunn. Further proof, if it were needed, that this was fast becoming a major incident. We were informed by the CO that the demonstrators now numbered in excess of 2,000. The town centre roads had been closed and a Muslim Cleric was conducting an inflammatory speech through a loud hailer on the steps of the Town Hall directly opposite the Bridewell. We were told that back up police units had been requested and were attending from neighbouring towns. Until they arrived we numbered less than fifty officers, several of whom had been pulled from desk jobs to boost the numbers. Our instructions were to enter the crowd and spread out to give the impression of much larger numbers and under no circumstances should we attempt to make any arrests. WHAT?? Was this guy straight out of kindergarten?

As instructed, out we went to mingle with the crowd, armed with a short wooden truncheon, set of handcuffs and a police radio. It wasn't possible to see your nearest colleague. Suicide. The protest had been ongoing for a couple of hours or so and things were heating up. I glanced at the guy on the steps who was repeating eerie chants through his mega phone. His tongue was bright red, apparently from a dye used to enhance the effects of the chants. I could swear his eyes were red too. It would have been easy to take this guy for the Devil himself. I was approached by one Asian man who was a similar age to myself at the time 21 or 22. He looked me in the eye and said "I bet you're scared for your life. You should be." I wasn't going to tell him, but I fuckin' was!!

Just then a message rippled through the crowd. The prisoners were not being released. Oh, wow, thanks for the heads up Chief! The crowd erupted like wild animals, running in every direction. Parked vehicles were smashed, turned over and set alite. Shop windows were destroyed with bricks, bottles and any other makeshift missiles close to hand. Our little cluster of officers was ordered back to the sanctuary of the nick. No arguments there! Having hastily returned to HQ and dusted down, we were given the information that several back up riot units had arrived and were taking to the streets. A quick swig of tea and we would join them.

It was mayhem. There were rioters running in every direction destroying everything before them, seemingly at random. Although still hugely outnumbered, it seemed we now had just enough units to make some arrests. This didn't sit well with the CO whose earlier instructions were being ignored and we were promptly ordered back to our nearby riot vans. While we were huddled in our vans catching our breath and gathering our thoughts, our unit Inspectors told us that our radios were now on open mic. This meant anything said into one radio would be heard on every other radio as CO Dunn prepared to address the troops.

In what can only be described as a dreadful attempt to emulate Winston Churchill in Bradford's hour of need, the CO began his delivery with a request for collective calm amongst the ranks. "Try telling the fuckers that are tearing the City apart," was the advice offered by one unconvinced bobby.

"Let me remind you all I am able to hear everything and I will not hesitate to take action against any officer who fails to conduct him or herself professionally". Jeers instantly rang out seemingly from every listener. This guy had no leadership skills at all and in the length of two sentences he had alienated the very men he should have been leading. "Right," Winston continued. "There will be no more warnings. I have heard reports from a number of officers that they have been targeted by the demonstrators with glass bottles and full drinks cans. Well, I am here to tell you that I have personally been patrolling the streets and at no time have I seen anything other than the occasional empty plastic bottle tossed into the air." "Well open your fuckin' eyes, you're a joke," was one response. "Grow a set of bollocks," was another. Each of which was met with hearty cheers of agreement, before we were instructed by a mysterious new voice to take to the streets and restore order.

The streets now resembled war-torn Lebanon. Cars were burning on street corners and buildings were devoid of any glazing.

Needless to say, numerous arrests followed and after several hours of chasing the ring leaders around the City centre, the rioters' numbers began to dwindle and something akin to normality returned to the streets.

It's not certain what happened to Winston but rumour had it that he left the force to become head of security at a local pensioners' home.

7

Down-Town Drop-Out

Radio call: attend report of 'sudden death'. (A term used to cover any type of reported death, the largest percentage resulting from natural causes). I was soon at the address, where I obtained details of the deceased from the next of kin, the wife of an elderly man who had been fighting prostate cancer, only to suffer the ignominy of passing away whilst on the toilet.

The lady identified the body to me, which I examined for any suspicious marks. Everything appeared in order (apart from he was dead) and at my request the undertakers arrived and placed the body into the private ambulance. I followed the ambulance as it made its way towards the town centre morgue where I would sign over the body for continuity.

All was looking good. My Friday night shift was almost done. But no! Too good to be true. As the ambulance turned into a dimly lit, seedy little back street with me in tow, I could see ahead a mass punch up. There appeared to be about twenty men involved some thirty yards further up the street. Hmmm, quick change of mind-set. I now found myself single-crewed in a marked police vehicle, outside my sub-divisional area. The significance there is that I now had to radio my control room who in turn would have to contact town centre operations, who would have to dispatch units to my location. That was assuming there would be anyone free to send on a typically busy Friday night in Bradford.

Okay, stay calm. I had appraised my control room so they would do the necessary. Right now, I needed a plan. Shit! I couldn't think of anything. I'd just have to wing it.

At that very moment, as if by divine intervention, the ambulance made a ninety degree turn, coming to a halt facing the mortuary shutter door. This served to temporarily block my progress and also provided a screen beyond which the brawlers would be unaware of my presence.

The shutter door was now being slowly raised. Come on man, think. Got it! Full beam headlights, blue flashing roof light and constant blasting of the car horn (no sirens on the panda car, huh).

The ambulance was moving into the morgue now and I could get through. This is it! I commenced my plan in style. A ripping wheel spin, which shot me forward towards the ensuing scrap, and a screeching handbrake stop as I reach the battle. Perfect - this has to look impressive. They can't know that I'm alone.

Right I'm out. Shit! No, I'm not. In my haste I had forgotten one important detail: my seat belt. As I launched myself from the vehicle, the belt allowed me only half an exit before snapping shut, leaving me dangling from the open door like a puppet, my head resting on the wet ground. Twat! A quick attempt to pull myself back into the car proved fruitless. In a freak twist of fate, my truncheon which was housed in my trouser sheath, had become wedged between the door well and the underside of the seat. I looked towards the crowd from my inverted position and realised that I had achieved my initial objective. I had brought the fight to a halt.

Unfortunately for me, it seemed I had united the two factions, for now they stood as one, their attention fully focused on my predicament as they laughed and jeered. What now? Yes, the cavalry are here, proceeded by the flashing blue lights and screaming sirens. I watched as the meat wagon sped around the corner and pulled up at the far end of the street. This had the thugs running in all directions with one individual in particular making a hasty move straight at me. Then darkness. I can only imagine what happened next but an educated guess would be that a well aimed boot from the assailant had smashed the door into my chin rendering me unconscious.

A short time later, having been released from my shackles and given the all clear, I made my way home whilst I considered the alternative implications of the road safety campaign: 'Clunk click every trip'.

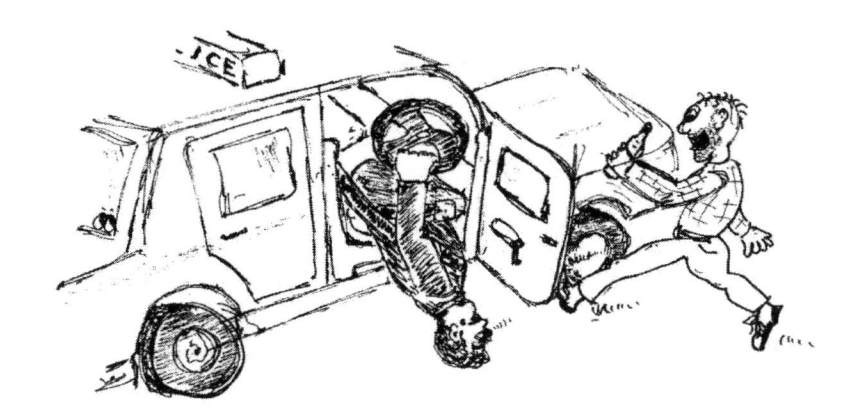

8

On The Job TRAIN-ing

Wrong place, wrong time for this one. I had just finished my meal break and was making my way from the canteen to the car park via the control room hatch.

"Oh Tim, great! Can you take a look at this for me?" Yelled Angie the control room operative. Turns out we'd had a call from British Rail. One of their drivers had reported running over what he thought was a tailor's dummy. Hmmm, it's not going to be a dummy, me thinks.

There was one good break however. Sitting in the control room was one of our seasoned Inspectors and top bloke to boot. Inspector Holls offered to accompany me to the given location and I was only too pleased to accept his offer.

We grabbed the Dragon lamp (basically a powerful torch which cast a very bright light considerably further than a standard torch) and we were on our way.

The 'tailor's dummy' was waiting for us inside a railway tunnel in the West Bowling area of Bradford. In a totally professional style, we stood by the entrance of the tunnel smoking our cigs while we made some calls to ensure there would be no trains running during our search. Two or maybe three cigs later we were given the okay to commence our journey. Dragon lamp on, deep breath and away we go.

It's cold, damp and has that musty smell and even with the lamp, visibility is not that great. From outside, the arched tunnel had looked quite large as it housed two parallel lines running in opposite directions. Now we were inside it felt strangely claustrophobic and intimidating. The echoes bounced off the Yorkshire stone walls and ceiling as we slowly crunched across the stone chippings beneath our boots. Nothing yet and we were a good hundred yards or more inside. A few yards further and as we looked back we could no longer see the tunnel opening. Then there it was, a short distance away a large bundle lay in the middle of the tracks.

Okay, let's see what we got. It was no tailor's dummy. Instead, as we feared, it was the body of a man, surprisingly not torn apart as we may have anticipated. In fact, he was almost unblemished. Well, apart from there being no head! We took a minute to gather our thoughts. The sight of a decapitated body enhancing the already intoxicating atmosphere. (I almost used the term 'heady atmosphere' though it doesn't seem apt here). In order to preserve any forensics evidence we were unable to move the body, instead we took a look around the immediate area.

Only a few feet away, inside one of the maintenance safety recesses we discovered a number of items which had been neatly laid out, presumably by our friend, prior to his demise. The presentation included a photograph of a man in his early 40s with a name and address on the reverse. Very considerate for assisting with identification. There was also a wedding ring, house door key, some loose change and a half empty can of pop. Everything was left in situ and we continued down the tunnel in search of the missing cranium.

On reaching the opening at the far end of the tunnel without locating the missing piece, we both reached for the fags before radioing the control room with an update. We were informed that the Detective Chief Inspector was en route with a number of detectives and we were instructed to make our way back down the tunnel to our original entry point.

Having finished our smokes we started the return journey following the beam of light from the Dragon lamp. Now here's a bit of a shocker for me and Mr Hollis. As we reached the body from this reverse angle, we can see that the head is not missing but is in fact hanging downwards along the back of the torso, attached to the neck and shoulders by a sliver of muscle and skin tissue and he was looking directly towards us, complete with spectacles!

It was at this point that the true desperation of this man became clear. He had obviously waited in the safety recess sipping on his canned drink until he heard the train approach. It was then he had walked to the centre of the tunnel where he had laid on the ground at ninety degrees to the tracks before placing his neck on the line in such a way as to face the on coming train while still wearing his glasses, wow!

Okay, out of the tunnel to our assembly point where we were greeted by the DCI and his team. After informing him of our findings, he took a look around the immediate area in front of the tunnel and to our horror announced that this is obviously where the deceased had entered; a deduction based on the large number cigarette butts scattered on the ground. Having glanced towards each other we quickly bagged the tabs for evidence without uttering a word.

The forensic team arrived and examined the scene, collecting physical evidence, photographs, etc. In an effort to be thorough the DCI decided it would be a good idea to do a full sweep of the tunnel assisted by the footlights offered by a shunting train, which had been dispatched to the scene. This was almost a great idea until the team of ten or twelve officers, which included me and Inspector Hollis, were a couple of hundred yards into the belly of the tunnel. It must have struck the team leader at this point that he had made a slight oversight, officers were either passing out or being sick as they were consumed by the diesel fumes pumping out of the lead train.

Final sweep done, evidence collected, body removed. However, the interest didn't end there as I was then dispatched to the address that had been handwritten on the rear of the photograph, together with the door key.

A search of the address some 20 miles away revealed a second body. This time a murder victim!

In the master bed on the first floor of the house lay the wife of the headless corpse. She had been strangled several days earlier. Evidence in the house suggested that someone had made a number of suicide attempts. Empty pill bottles lay on the bedroom carpet alongside dried pools of vomit. A TV type coax cable dangled from the open loft hatch. The cable had extendeded to such a length that a person of average height attempting to hang themselves in this manner would have merely been lowered gently to the ground as the cable stretched.

Having discovered both bodies and located all the evidence, the case was then concluded by detectives from Wakefield as the series of events had originated within their divisional boundaries. In effect, having done all the dirty work, we had handed them an open-and-shut case.

All in a day's work to a degree, however, what did stick in my throat was the lack of acknowledgement from the coroner. Not only had me and Inspector Hollis done all the initial work, I then had to stand up in a Coroner's Court and recount all the details of both bodies and their corresponding circumstances in front of members from both the deceased's families. Okay, that's the job but here's the thing – at the conclusion of the hearing, the coroner asked the two Wakefield Detective Inspectors to stand in court before awarding them both with a commendation for their outstanding work. What!!!

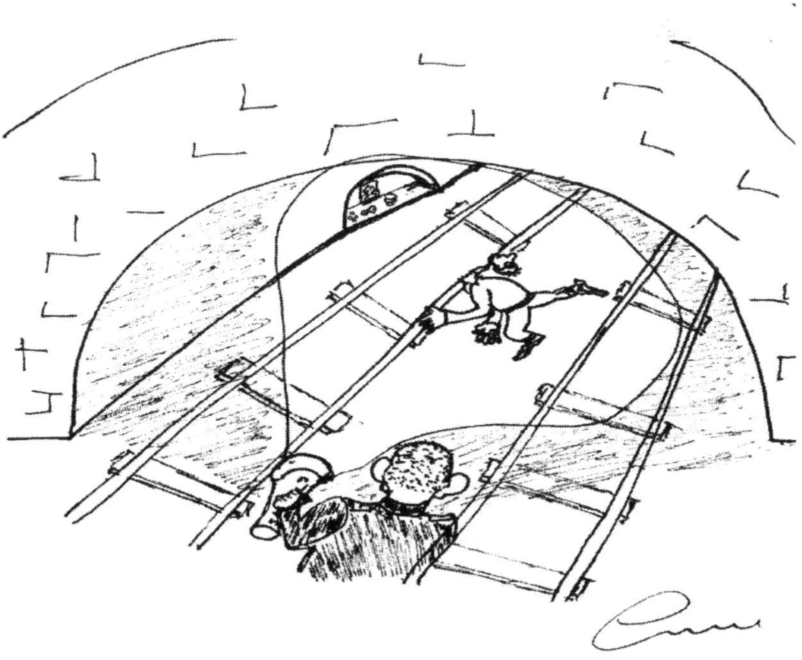

9

Tipsy Tory

One afternoon shift Jane and I were instructed to return home and get brushed up and put on our best civilian suits before attending a learning centre for mentally and physically impaired adults in West Bowling.

Jane was the station pinup, platinum blonde, petite, Olympic standard swimmer. Enough said.

It turned out there was to be an impromptu visit to the centre by a member of parliament in recognition of them winning a government award.

Having arrived at the premises we liaised with members of staff appraising them of our presence before taking up a position on the main carpark close to the entrance. Our brief was to act as a discrete form of plain clothed police presence, if such a thing is possible.

Right on queue, a shiny black Daimler saloon car with blacked out windows pulled up into the carpark. The company directors stood to the side of the entrance door ready to welcome the MP. Jane and I remained a few yards away in what we considered a relatively unobtrusive spot, still not really sure why we were there.

As we continued to ponder, four large chaps in black suits and ties stepped out of the car, three of them positioning themselves around the Daimler whilst the forth opened the rear passenger door. Out stepped the incredibly tall and thin bespectacled MP who we shall call Mr H. His first step onto terra firma was not at all convincing as he staggered to his right only prevented from toppling over by one of his security officers taking hold of his upper arm. Not wishing to appear incapable, Mr H shrugged off the hand of his aide and made a b-line towards me. I would swear he had consumed a few sherries but in the interest of avoiding a lawsuit I'm prepared to say its possible he had just returned from a lengthy trip at sea. He swayed towards me with a large grin on his face, stopping with his size 14 shoe resting on my toe. He thrust out his right hand gesturing for a hand shake which I reciprocated, taking the opportunity to prevent him toppling forward onto me.

With a slight slur in his voice he said, "It's a pleasure to meet you. I hope I haven't kept you waiting." I assured him everything was fine before introducing myself and Jane.

There was a smell on his breath that had me doubting my previous thoughts regarding the sea trip. We were all spared any further embarrassment when the original security officer again took hold of Mr H. by his arm and ushered him towards the two directors waiting by the front door.

"This way Mr H. The people we are here to meet are right this way."

I watched as Mr H. reached the intended welcoming party and two of the other body guards took over the responsibility of keeping him upright as they guided him inside the building, allowing the first agent to return to us.

"I'm sorry about that," he said. "He's emptied the cocktail bar in the back of the car while we were driving here."

It wasn't a problem to me or Jane, in fact far from it. I had never met a Senior MP before and he seemed like a top bloke. Who doesn't like a drink or three? On chatting further with the bodyguard, he confirmed he was a member of MI5 and he and the rest of his team were indeed all carrying firearms. This was real James Bond material.

The following minutes flew by as the agent indulged us with some of the events he had been involved in and it wasn't long before Mr H. reappeared from the Centre and once again headed straight over to Jane and I. Still wearing the same smile he had arrived with he said, "Thank you both so much. It's been an absolute pleasure," before he tottered off to his car where the rear door was being held open by the senior agent, who threw us a wink before he and Mr H. took their seats in the car, which was driven off at speed.

What a top bloke!

10

Valley Parade – The Fire

(Bradford City Football Club)

Without doubt, this is my most difficult subject to recall, though not in the obvious way you would imagine.

Saturday, 11th May 1985 was the last game of the season with Bradford City already having won the old division 4 title the week before. Their opponents were mid-table Lincoln City and this was to be a day of celebration in front of their highest crowd of the season (a little over 11,000) with the club captain receiving the league trophy just before kick off at 3pm.

I am passionate about football and would rarely miss an opportunity to work at any of the numerous grounds within a small radius of Bradford. On that terrible day in question, I was rostered to be on duty at the game but I chose to take a day's leave to play cricket. Singularly the biggest regret of my life.

At 2pm that afternoon I donned my whites and took to the field to play a league match for my local village team. The irony is that I'm not a real cricketer. I could give the ball a whack but mainly I enjoyed a laugh with the lads and a beer or four after the game. It was a lovely warm day, though fairly windy, and I was fielding in my customary position close to the boundary edge, as far as possible from the action, in the captain's words.

It must have been just before 4pm when my dad, Bert, arrived to watch the game as he often did although this time would be different. His opening words to me and anyone else close enough to hear was that a local radio station had reported that a fire had started inside the Bradford City football ground. It registered with me as I should have been there. However, most of the other players shrugged it off thinking perhaps that when it was dealt with, Bradford would probably get a nice new stadium. My dad watched the cricket for a few minutes before making his way home, just a short walk away. It wasn't long before Bert returned to the cricket ground and this time his words were fully attention grabbing- as my dad began to inform me that people were believed to have died at Valley Parade.

The cricket game came to a grinding halt and the pitch emptied as everyone gathered to glean more information. The only real update was that the emergency services were in attendance and battling to control the fire, which had engulfed the main stand within minutes of it starting. Aware that people were now in need of more information, my dad again headed for home and the much sought after update.

The cricket game had been abandoned by now and lads were just milling around offering their thoughts as to what may have caused the fire and what the extent of the damage might be. None of us were prepared for the news brought by Bert some 30 minutes later. The death toll was believed to be in the teens and rising. I went straight to my Dad's house and watched the recorded footage complete with a harrowing running commentary by ITV's John Helm.

Like everyone else, I was in complete shock. I rang a number of my colleagues who I knew had been at the ground and listened in disbelief at their first hand accounts. I then rang my station. I had to be there. After speaking to my duty inspector, I was instructed to attend the ground. An hour or so later, having grabbed my uniform, I was entering what was left of Valley Parade.

My brief was to act as security and public liaison. My shift began with a tour of the stadium. It was overwhelming. The smell was overpowering and the sight of the burnt out main stand was difficult to take in. Just hours earlier it had been packed with joyous fans-men, women and children celebrating their team's success. The forensic officer who showed me around explained that it was believed the fire had started close to the upper tier of the main stand, which had been completely engulfed in flames within four minutes of the fire starting, mainly due to the dried out wooden seats, roof timbers and the bitumen coverings that had showered molten tar onto the unfortunate souls below. He went on to explain that the burning bitumen had billowed out thick black smoke, which had rendered breathing and visibility to almost zero. The heat could only be measured by the injuries of those who had escaped the fire by running to the front of the stand and onto the pitch. Though the majority these fans had survived, video footage shows several of these people with their hair and clothing spontaneously bursting into flame. The majority of those who died appeared to have panicked in the overwhelming conditions and, fearing for their lives, had instinctively run to the top of the stand towards the exit doors and turnstiles.

Those who made it that far found the exits and turnstiles locked. By this time they would have been exhausted, disorientated and overcome with the smoke, and perished where they lay.

The forensics officer returned to his duties and I was left to wander the stand alone trying to make sense of what had happened. Immediately my attention was drawn to a body crumpled and disfigured and covered in hardened bitumen, which would have showered down in molten form from the roof covering above, leaving the deceased in almost the same seated position from which they would have been enjoying their last game of football. I took a moment to try and imagine how this could happen. Why you wouldn't even try to move, to survive. Maybe they were lucky-a heart attack or struck on the head by falling debris. Something swift; something which spared at least some of the horror. I dragged myself away. Already unsure I wanted to see any more but I was compelled to go on.

Then on the concrete walkway close to the top of the main stand I saw the ash covered bodies. Though not immediately identifiable, recognizable enough to know that this was an adult with his arms stretched out around his two children in a last defiant act to protect them from the inferno.

In the days and weeks following the fire, lists of those who had perished were published in the local press adding probable names to accompany the harrowing picture which will stay with me forever.

I forced myself towards the top of the stand where more than 20 charred bodies are stacked on top of each other pressed against one of the locked doors. A little further along were more crushed and twisted bodies trapped part way through and below the locked turnstiles as they tried to force their way to safety. The concrete toilet block contained yet more bodies, better preserved than those outside who were fully exposed to the flames and debris. These poor souls must have stumbled in through the blackness via the door sized opening, believing for the briefest moment that they had, against all the odds, successfully navigated a way out of the stadium, only to crash into the solid rear wall which effectively sealed their fate.

In all, 56 people perished that terrible day along with the 265 who suffered serious burns and the countless numbers who will carry mental scars for the rest of their lives.

I wasn't there when I should have been and the overwhelming feeling of sadness and despair that consumed me that day was undoubtedly a major reason for my nervous breakdown some six years later, when I was medically retired from the force.

The people of Bradford must be respected for the manner in which they came together and conducted themselves both at the time of this terrible disaster and during the many painful years since.

May the victims rest in peace. I'm so sorry I couldn't help.

11

Metro v Cosworth

Many of you will be aware of the recent cutbacks to police funding which has only served to stretch the thin blue line even further. The sight of the community bobby patrolling the streets is already a fading memory. However, cut backs are not restricted exclusively to the modern era.

Around the early 1980s British car company Austin launched the Mini Metro essentially designed as a cheap, compact, fuel efficient run-around. The reality transpired to be considerably different to the dream. The resulting product resembled a hideous crossbreed between a child's pushchair and a shopping trolley and included the same tiny wheels and handling characteristics.

Internally this car was, to say the least, cramped and under the bonnet it boasted the acceleration of an old man on a bicycle. Not the ideal vehicle for transporting hairy arsed coppers you would think. Wrong! At least according to the police authority who, having looked at the price tag, ordered a shed load.

Around the same time, and in sharp contrast to our new flagship, another car company, namely Ford, released a thoroughbred beast in the form of a Sierra Cosworth. This king of the road produced over 200bhp and had the handling ability of a rally car. Not surprisingly this became an instant favourite with the car thieves and joyriders.

On one particular night shift, I was partnered with Ned, (A nickname derived from his uncanny resemblance to the Australian outlaw 'Ned Kelly') Ned was a young lad fairly new to the job but a natural. Built like a kick boxer with a blonde crew cut and fearless mentality, his unassuming and warm nature made him great company.

As you have already guessed, on this particular night we had drawn the short straw and here we were parked up in the Metro. It's 3am and we are on a narrow, badly lit road on the outskirts of the Holmewood council estate where we had chosen to use the lull in activity to catch up with some paperwork. As we were busily scribbling away, the police radio shattered the silence with a message to all units. "Be aware that a Ford Sierra Cosworth has been stolen from the Holmewood area within the last 20 minutes." As we were only a short distance from where the stolen car was last seen, I quipped to Ned how funny it would be if it came our way. As I uttered the words Neds eyes shot out on stalks for there in the distance were a set of full beam headlights coming towards us at speed.

We were like two schoolboys, cheering and hooping as I cranked the Metro into life. The Cosworth thundered by us but I was able to recognize the driver as a young man I had arrested previously for the offence of TWLA (taking a motor vehicle without lawful consent). It was at this point that I discovered another wonderful feature of the Metro, its turning circle, which is best compared to that of a cruise ship. As I made a fifteen point manoeuvre, my mate kept his eyes in the direction of the stolen Sierra whilst radioing in our sighting. Our objective here was simple, in fact no, it wasn't. It was almost bloody impossible. We needed to keep the Cosworth in sight long enough for the rapid response vehicles to reach the area. As we lurched forward Ned gave me a running commentary, graphically detailing my upcoming manoeuvres in the same manner as a rally co-driver. Well, left, right and straight on at least. This was never likely to be one of the lengthiest vehicle pursuits in policing history. Yet to our credit, and I guess the Metro too, we clung onto the Sierra's taillights away in the distance (a long, long way into the distance) just long enough for the traffic cops to arrive.

Now the fight was a fair one. It didn't take long before the Cosworth careered through a garden wall, coming to rest on someone's front lawn.

The two occupants managed to escape on foot, but as I knew who they were it wouldn't be long before they were tracked down. Sure enough the crime report for the stolen Sierra was allocated to me within a couple of days of the incident.

On the night in question I had gained a clear view of the driver, a young man we shall refer to as Blamewares. Here was a guy in his mid twenties who already had an extensive record for stealing cars and house burglaries. Blamewares was a big lad who had built himself a reputation as a hard man. So I grabbed my own hard man in the form of Ned and we set off to the suspect's address in Bierley, one of the many council estates within our subdivision. I had also arranged for a response car to meet us at the location in the event of Blamewares repeating his previous performance. It proved to be a fairly prudent move as the instant I stopped the patrol car outside his address, Blamewares came flying down his garden path and began running away down the middle of the road.

I had barely applied the hand brake before Ned was out of the car and hot footing it after our suspect. I quickly joined the chase and could see ahead that the other two officers had left their vehicle and were moving to cut off Blamewares as he fled in their direction. There followed several minutes of dodging backwards and forwards before Ned got close enough to launch a well aimed rugby tackle around Blamewares legs, bringing him crashing to the ground. As spectacular as this was, it palled into oblivion compared to the belly flop onto Blamewares chest performed by the fattest copper I've ever seen. This move expelled all the air from his lungs in the form of a blood curdling scream, effectively bringing the proceedings to a fairly tame ending, for us at least. The response lads scraped up Blamewares and escorted him to their car and subsequently the Bridewell.

I gave Ned a pat on the back as we made our way back to the patrol car, where I could see the back doors were wide open. A quick look on the back seat and I could see both our helmets had been stolen. A full scale search for the missing helmets proved unnecessary as just five yards from us, leaning on his gate post was Blamewares dad. "Lost anything lads?" He enquired of us in a sarcastic manner. "Hope its not your helmets, you'd probably lose your jobs for that!" He continued letting out a raucous belly laugh, clearly impressed with his own opportunist theft and witty repartee.

I told Blamewares Snr to go get the helmets and almost too easily he turned and walked into his house, reappearing moments later carrying the two police helmets. As anticipated it had never been his intention to hand over the helmets so easily, infact he just wanted to taunt us further. "Let my lad go and you can have your stupid hats back" he demanded. I wasn't in the mood for sub standard comedy, so having asked nicely, I exchanged a kick in his balls for the helmets. "Now you're nicked like sonny boy." Two Blamewares for the price of one. Good day.

Before I move on a final mention for the Metro. Although it remained as part of the fleet for the best part of five years officers never tired in their efforts to avoid being handed the reins. Taking any evasive action necessary, including hiding the keys prior to roll call. Of course there would always be a loser and on one particular evening two colleagues from my station, but a different team, drew the short straw. The bobby's assigned the Metro couldn't possibly have imagined what lay in store for them. Just a few hours later as they responded to a 999 emergency call, a young man with a long history of depression was finishing his last pint of beer inside a pub situated on Bierley Lane, while he contemplated his suicide. In a strange twist of fate as the young man left the pub and began walking along the pavement the Metro which was displaying its full headlights, flashing blue roof light and sounding its siren, came speeding towards him. Desperate times often lead to desperate measures and sadly the young guy felt he couldn't go on any longer and with impeccable timing he threw himself into the path of the oncoming Metro. The impact from his body crushed the bonnet, shattered the windscreen, and created a deep vee shape in the roof as he was thrown over the back of the car. He died instantly and both the officers inside the vehicle required hospital treatment, though neithers injuries were long term. As for the Metro, it was subjected to a thorough forensic examination before being retired from service and scrapped.

12

More From The Square

There were many incidents relating to Newby Square and the closer it came to being demolished the more it attracted criminals of all types from the opportunist looking for scrap wiring and metal, water boilers, sinks, kitchen units, anything which could be removed from the vacated flats and turned into a bit of cash for the weekends drug fix. It also became a favourite spot for abandoning stolen cars, hiding stolen goods, and dealing drugs. In 1985 less than 20 years after being built it was claimed that the flats were being felled due to structural defects, this was probably the main reason but it was also a golden opportunity to disperse the criminal element from what had become known locally as Fort Apache the Bronx. The first problem we faced as the tower blocks were slowly leveled was the ever increasing piles of bricks and rubble or as the natives saw it a lovely stock pile of ammo conveniently located to dispel our attempts to enter the square. During the best part of the two years which it took to completely remove the square it became increasingly necessary to use undercover officers in the area to combat the rising level of crimes. Coppers wearing their scruffiest civillian clothes would be deployed at various times of the day and night to wander around the area nabbing members of the tea leaf army.

During one such patrol I was taking a breather leaning against the metal railings on a second floor walkway leading to a number of the last remaining dwellings. As I stood there drawing on my fag, wearing a pair of old ripped jeans, zipped up wind cheater, scruffy woolen hat and a pair of white Reebok training shoes I was approached by a young lad probably aged around 16 years of age. He was openly carrying a video recorder and seemingly without a care in the world and oblivious to who I was he asked me if I wanted to buy the VHS recorder, cheap. "Not sure I need one of those pal. What else you got?" I enquired. The lads eyes lit up and he asked me to follow as he led me into a nearby flat. I followed as he pushed open the front door and marched along the hallway towards the rear of the flat. A womans voice shouted out from the living room "Who the fuck is that?" "Its Addy, I've got a buyer for some of the gear" The lad replied, before continuing into what I presumed used to be a bedroom. As proud as punch he smiled towards me. "Anything you fancy mate I will do it cheap." It was all I could do not to laugh outloud. It was like Aladdins cave, there were TV,s, video's, radios, all manner of electrical items along with a couple of bicycles. "Wow you've got some great gear there my friend" I assured him. "I reckon I could shift some of that for you. Just hang fire while I go get my mate, see if he's got any cash on him." I left the lad punching the air in delight as I walked a short distance from his flat until I was out of ear shot. As quietly as I could I radioed my control room and requested a police van to attend, a patrol car wasn't going to be big enough for this haul. On returning to the flat I found my new friend still smiling like a Cheshire cat. "No worries pal, we're on. My mates getting some cash together, he wont be long." A bit of small talk followed before true to my word a few minutes later two of my uniformed mates appeared at the door. "You bastard ! You're the filth," was all my little mate could offer before making a half hearted dash for freedom. No way out. The two uniformed cops blocking the door hole made sure of that.

Still all's fair in love and war.

The young entrepreneur was arrested and later charged with various counts of burglary, theft and handling stolen goods. Whilst the majority of the recovered items held little value they still belonged to someone and after a bit of digging most of them were reunited with their rightful owners.

13

Crushed Emotions

Not all police work is fueled with danger and excitement, indeed the vast majority of calls could be described as routine, even mundane. Sometimes though the routine jobs could throw in a twist that would make them a little more memorable.

Such a call started when a 50-year-old man was crushed beneath a three tonne piece of engineering machinery. Though I didn't attend the scene, it was relayed to me that this accident occurred whilst the equipment was being hoisted across the workshop, some 20 feet in the air. It seems that as the machinery was being manoeuvred across the warehouse, a fault on the bindings allowed the metal bulk to come crashing down directly onto the victim below, killing him instantly.

My part in this tragedy was to be the bearer of the news to the deceased's widow. It was never an easy or pleasant task to stand in front of someone and tell them their loved one wouldn't be coming home. The circumstances of this man's death only added to the difficulty of the task in hand.

On my arrival outside the family home I could quickly see this was a well kept, clean semi-detached house. I rang the bell on the front door as in my head I ran through a few versions of how I might break the news to the spouse. A minute or two passed without response so I gave it the old-fashioned bobby's knock. Still no one answered but this time I was sure I had heard a noise from behind the door. Strange! I gave it another go, only this time as I knocked I held open the letterbox, which allowed me to see into the hallway.

Knock, knock. There she was! I had to take a double check at what I had just seen. Right on cue with my knocking, a very slender middle aged woman had darted from the living room across the hallway and disappeared through a small door under the staircase. I kept the letterbox flap open and attempted to draw the woman out from her hiding place but despite repeated efforts to identify myself and reassure her that she was in no danger, the lady made no response and refused to leave her sanctuary.

Why was this lady so nervous and timid? At the time there were details, important details, which I was unaware of. Most notably the lady was Polish and spoke no English. Perhaps this was something I should have been made aware of prior to my visit. Additionally, and probably more relevant to her current situation, we later learned that since moving from Poland some ten years previously, this lady had become almost totally dependent on her husband for even the most minor tasks, to the point where she seldom, if ever, left the house alone.

Following a chat with the duty Inspector, it was agreed that a female police officer would be of assistance. Having arrived at the house it took a considerable length of time before the PW managed to convince the distressed woman to open the door. Unfortunately, the problems didn't end there as due to the language barrier, we had to call for a translator, all of which could only have added to this woman's distress. Thankfully later that same day she was united with members of her family from the Midlands.

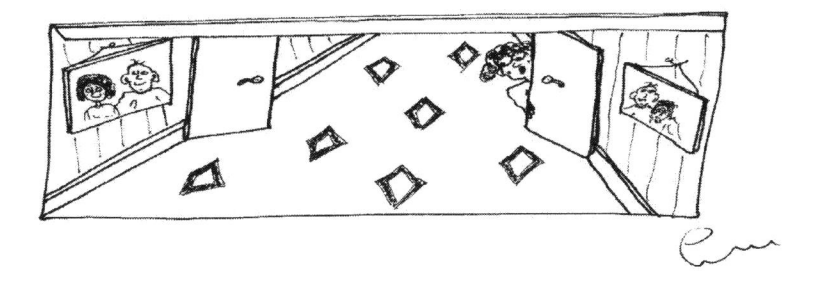

14

By Hukka by Crook

There is a great saying, 'people in glass houses shouldn't throw stones'. Here was a good example. Midday, foot patrol in my designated community area of West Bowling. Radio call, "Can you attend a report of kids playing football in the street." Great! Call me Dirty Harry. Best check my .44 Magnum is fully loaded for this one.

It was only a few streets away, so I was outside the caller's house in a matter of minutes. No sign of kids or a ball. Maybe they saw me coming. Maybe they were never here at all. Who knows.

I was greeted at the door by a young Asian woman who appeared to speak little English and I was directed into the living room with the aid of hand signals. Now there comes a time when you are allowed to think you have seen most things but how wrong could I be!

As I entered the room, I was overwhelmed by a thick, pungent smelling cloud of smoke. As I stared through the haze I could make out five large, middle aged Asian men wearing traditional dress, sitting cross legged on the floor around a low table in the centre of the room.

Initially no one looked my way or seemed to be aware of my presence, as they passed what appeared to be a Hukka pipe between themselves. Each of the men readily inhaled from the pipe before expelling more smoke into the already choking atmosphere. I let out a loud cough, partly to clear my lungs, but mainly to alert the gathering to my entrance. Nothing. The glass vessel was holding pride of place and I was merely a spectator to the proceedings.

I have to confess to being slightly shocked at their apparent total disregard at having a fully uniformed police officer present at what appeared to be a drugs party. It seemed the best course of action was to play dumb and see how things worked out. I said "I believe you've had a problem with some local youths?" Without a head being turned I was met with a tirade of abuse, albeit in broken English, from a man who appeared to be the Master of Ceremonies. The gist of his onslaught was to suggest that at best the police were disinterested and more likely totally unconcerned at any problems the Asian community may have.

After several exchanges of ideas, during which time the contents of the pipe continued to be drained, it was clear that nothing substantial could be offered to corroborate the alleged 'nuisance' or the culprits involved. I suggested at that point that it might be beneficial if I called a number of my colleagues who may be able to assist. As there appeared little or no reaction to my suggestion, I continued to make my call. I did in actual fact make a request for any available drug squad officers to attend the address to assess the contents of the Hukka pipe.

Luck was clearly on my side as detectives from the drug unit were in the area and within minutes two officers were on the scene. Their specialist knowledge quickly allowed them to identify the contents of the pipe as an illegal substance. A search of the house was then carried out, during which further small quantities of illegal drugs were discovered. As a result, the five men were arrested and transported to the local station along with the drugs.

Following the subsequent interviews, the men were cautioned for minor drug related offences after which the drugs were seized and destroyed. The moral of this story: 'Don't take the piss'.

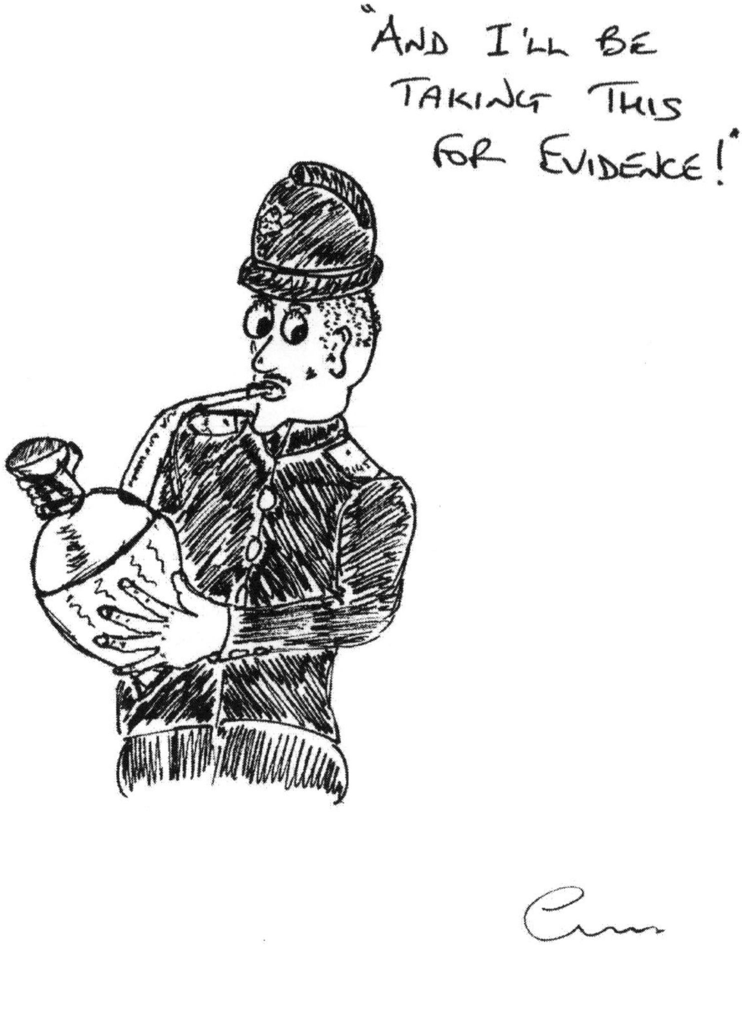
"AND I'LL BE TAKING THIS FOR EVIDENCE!"

15

Ned and the Scrap Yard Tealeaf

Sunday afternoon. Pretty quiet but you never could tell what might happen. The radio broke the tranquillity: "Passer-by reports a guy is loading scrap metal onto a flat-back wagon from a scrapyard off Wakefield Road." On the face of it, that didn't sound too suspicious until you factor in that the scrapyard in question was not open for business.

Okay, let's take a look. This would be a good run-out for Ned. Ned's the young gun at the nick. Best equipped for the 'action' end of the job so not wise to keep him cooped up in a car for longer than necessary.

We made our way to the scrapyard and swung off the duel carriageway, which is Wakefield Road, and onto a driveway that led up a slope to the yard's entrance gates. As the incline swept to the right, we found ourselves some 10 yards behind the flat-back wagon, which appeared fully loaded as it pumped out plumes of black diesel smoke as though ready for the off.

I placed the handbrake on and we both jumped out to assess the situation. However, as we stepped out of our vehicle the would-be thief threw open the driver's door of the wagon and leapt to the ground before running towards Wakefield Road. It seemed he was not as considerate as me as he'd chosen not to apply his handbrake. I could only watch as the tonnage of a metal-laden wagon rumbled backwards before crashing into the front of the stationary police vehicle. The sound of breaking glass and twisting metal was a great catalyst for Ned who was off like an Olympic sprinter in pursuit of a personal-best. The PB in this case was a slim built white male in his early 20s whose mop of black hair was flowing behind him as he hared away from the yard. So we were off, mop-top led the way closely followed by Ned, with baldy bringing up the rear. Moppit, as if wearing blinkers, ran out into the first lane of the westbound duel carriageway without a care for any oncoming traffic. Straight across the second lane before hurdling the heavy metal central safety barrier, pausing briefly to see if it might fit on his wagon. No time, so over the barrier and into the eastbound carriageway, the blinkers still serving to obscure the threat of oncoming cars.

Ned, though not blinkered, was displaying a serious case of tunnel vision and courage above-and-beyond the call of duty. He sped across the lanes of traffic and over the hurdles with unwavering determination, matching mop-top stride for stride.

My role in this pursuit was that of an observer, seemingly the only one aware that the race was across a well used duel carriageway. My decision to stay on the yard side of the road however, turned out to be a useful one.

On the opposite side of the thoroughfare was a heavily wooded park. I watched as the two runners reached the trees before the pacesetter made a U turn and dashed back onto the carriageway. This was my cue and I readied myself to grab him as he crossed to my side of the road, still hotly pursued by Ned. No such luck! I was clocked by Moppet who was in no mood to quit. He dipped a shoulder and spun on his heels back across the road in the direction of the trees.

As I glanced at Ned clambering over the central reservation his face told me that he really didn't like this guy. Still, this race was not over. Time I got involved and gave my pal a lift. At this point in the chase anyone watching from the sidelines must surely have been making comparisons to the Keystone Cops, or a Benny Hill chase without the lovely ladies. Not for much longer though for as Ned's patience was starting to run as thin as my breathing, the lead runner went for a change of plan and having cleared the second carriageway, he took off at speed into the wooded park.

This proved to be his worse decision yet and a great result for us. Because as he was pounding through the trees closely followed by Ned, who was shouting messages of goodwill, his concentration waned and he turned to respond to the encouragement, momentarily averting his eyes from the solid branch just inches away from his head. Crunch, right across the temple, followed by a short silence as he sailed backwards through the air. Finally, a thud as he landed unceremoniously on his back, quite literally out for the count. Strike one and a great collar for the new kid on the block.

16

Anonymous call

I had been pushing for a place in the CID (Crime Investigation Department) for some time and had recently accompanied detectives on a number of minor cases. Whilst working an afternoon shift in uniform, I was approached by DC Johns with a view to keeping observations on a local Asian general store. This would probably be an inconvenience for the CID and perhaps not the best use of their time. For me, it was the exact opposite. Conducting observations was one of my preferred engagements and it couldn't do my application any harm.

Everything had to be done at the double quick as an anonymous call had been received alleging that a large distribution warehouse in Wales had been broken into several hours earlier. Enquiries were made with the police in Wales and it was confirmed that a large warehouse had indeed been the subject of a major burglary. The caller had continued to reveal that a large quantity of the stolen goods would be making their way to Bradford with a general store being the intended destination, adding that the items would be transported in a dark coloured Ford Transit style van.

My instructions were to grab my civvy jacket to wear over my uniform, take an unmarked police vehicle and park up in a location were I would have a good view of the said shop. So, there I was parked up some 200 yards from the shop front with little to do but wait and hope.

The 10 PM shift changeover came and went without incident, now there was a new radio control room operator overseeing the night staff. None of this was likely to affect me, or so I thought.

A couple of hours passed and just around midnight a dark blue Ford Transit van came into view. Wow! The hairs on my neck stood straight. This tip off was looking really good. Sure enough, exactly as the informant had suggested, the van was driven off the road onto the driveway alongside the shop. Two Asian males stepped out from the front of the vehicle and opened the sliding side door of the van from where a further two Asian males exited. The second two males were each carrying large packages wrapped in clear cling film beneath which could be seen quantities of 200 packs of cigarettes. I immediately radioed the control room with my call sign (simply my four digit service number). "What are you still doing on duty? We thought you had gone off at 10pm." Bloody hell! No one from my shift, or the C.I.D had bothered to tell the night staff where I was, or what I was doing. No time to go into detail now as I could see cartons being unloaded from the van as I spoke. So to keep it short and swift I asked for two backup units to be dispatched to my location urgently. "Will do, as soon as a unit becomes available. Everyone is tied up at the moment."

As brief as I could make it, I informed control ops of the situation, before leaving my vehicle and taking the short walk to the store. I couldn't take the risk of waiting for other units to arrive as the stolen goods would become impossible to identify if the cartons were removed from the shrink wrap, due to the batch numbers only being attached to the exterior covering. I was on my way to the van. It was unlikely I was going to fool anyone with my civvy jacket, which did nothing to hide my sharp pressed black trousers and shiny black Doc Martin boots.

In the most casual manner I could muster, I ambled up the driveway and past the open door on the side of the van. The two men I had originally seen carrying packages from the vehicle were now back inside the van and appeared unaware or unconcerned by my presence and continued to busy themselves moving further parcels towards the opening. I continued on and walked straight through an open door, which led into the side of the shop where the plunder appeared to be heading. It was almost surreal as I stood and watched a further four men beavering away stacking the treasures against the walls of the storage area attached to the main building.

Bizzarely, as I stood there, a barely disguised white police officer in half uniform rubbing shoulders with the Asian occupants. Not one of them chose to challenge my intrusion or indeed usher me away from their activities. It was understandable in some respects as time was of the essence and they needed to disperse the stolen goods as quickly as possible. In an effort to play for time whilst other units reached me, I laughingly attempting to make small talk with classic lines such as "Big delivery you've got there fellas," and "working late tonight lads?" Still nothing. It was crazy. I was out numbered like Custer in his last stand. I could have been bundled into the van and never seen again but, luckily for me, these guys were just totally preoccupied with the job before them. On reflection, the alternatives to the way this eventually played out, were mind numbing.

Not before time, the troops arrived. A couple of patrol cars and DCs Johns and Morph. Six men were arrested at the scene and the stolen goods, which, along with the cigarettes included cigars, wine and cases of bottled spirits, were recovered to the police evidence room. Well, it was a make shift evidence room due to the huge quantity of items.

While the suspects were processed at the Bridewell, I was invited to catalogue the goodies. Gee thanks lads! There were literally thousands of items, which were given a final value in excess of £50,000. A solid connection was established linking everything to the original burglary in Wales and interviews with those in custody were commenced, resulting in further arrests during the following days and weeks. Pride of place amongst the arrests was a man identified as being the main link between the original burglary and the distribution throughout the county of West Yorkshire.

Numerous charges were brought against those arrested, which resulted in a total collection of fifteen years behind bars.

Like everything in life, nothing is ever quite so simple and unbeknown to me at the time, an hour or so after I was expected home from my evening shift, my loving wife had called the station, initially concerned regarding my welfare and enquiring as to my whereabouts. Due to the lack of information at the shift handover, my wife was told that to the best of their knowledge I had signed off at 10pm. As I didn't make it home until some 12 hours later, to this day she struggles to accept that I was ever involved in what remains one of the most satisfying cases of my career. I guess sometimes you just can't win. I wonder where she thought I could be?

17

When is a chair not a chair

It was mobile patrol duties today and for company in my vehicle I had the platinum blonde, blue eyed, station pinup.

Everyone has their Achillies heel and the expression 'dizzy blonde' would accurately describe Jane's. We had attended one or two routine calls when we were dispatched to a ground floor flat located in the Holmewood council estate, which at the time was the largest in Europe. We were informed that a neighbour had found the occupant, a man in his late 70s, dead, though there appeared to be no suspicious circumstances.

As we drove to the flat I remembered how I had attended the same address several weeks earlier regarding kids throwing stones at the windows. My recollection of this visit was vivid as the smell inside the property was practically unbearable. En route, I attempted to give Jane the heads-up on just how horrendous the stench was but despite my best efforts I could see my words were falling on deaf ears and she was fully focused on the job in hand.

As we pulled up outside the flat and began walking towards the door, memories of how atrocious the smell had been hit me hard and my legs refused to take me past the already open front door. Jane however, still oblivious to the fate awaiting her, entered the property crossing the narrow passage leading to the kitchen and walked forward into the lounge. My position by the front door, half in and out of the opening, gave me an unobstructed view and this is where I would remain as even here the pungent smell was scorching my nostrils. I could see from my vantage point that the deceased who was laid on a sofa, was indeed the same old boy I had seen on my previous visit. Jane was now standing over the body in the living room (living room seems strangely inappropriate in these circumstances, so we will stick with lounge), and her hand was pressed to her face as she visibly struggled to hang on to her breakfast.

In a desperate bid for fresh air, she dashed to the far wall of the room and flung open one of the four feet tall metal framed windows. Nothing changed, the solid block of stagnant air that filled the lounge refused to leave and the air outside was barred from entering. Jane was by now fully aware of her predicament and the 'dizzy blonde' syndrome started to kick in. Yet in defiance to the overwhelming circumstances, she continued with her duties and began taking notes from the neighbour. Whilst juggling between note taking and breathing, the lounge rapidly began to fill with grieving friends and relatives of the deceased and their collective wailing and moaning became almost comical in the choking smell.

Jane was aware that seating was at a premium and in addition to consoling everyone, she was now chasing around the flat searching for chairs or indeed anything that could be used for the same purpose. Within minutes it appeared that all seating aides, chairs, stools, buffets and alike had been located and put to purpose. The front room was by now wall-to-wall packed with well wishers all grieving uncontrollably.

The scene was set for the grand finale' and as if not to miss such a spectacle, the two undertakers arrived right on cue joining me by the entrance door and soaking in the intoxicating smells and sights before them. Just when it seemed there could be no one left to attend, an elderly lady bustled her way into the hall. Not to be beaten at this late stage Jane rushed to the old woman and promised to find her a chair. True to her word Jane span round on her heels glancing around the various rooms before coming to a halt with the eyes fixed on the opening to the kitchen. "Oh no" was the instruction chanted by my little trio as we glanced towards the kitchen, for there indeed stood a chair. Only this was no ordinary chair.

The remainder of the audience appeared oblivious to what was about to take place as they continued their out-pouring alongside the body. It was now over to Jane to bring the curtain down. Despite repeated warnings from myself and my boys, not to touch the chair, her mind was set as she darted towards the kitchen. In a single motion the chair was hoisted into the air to shoulder height as she turn to guide it through the narrow hallway. This last remaining chair was in fact a commode and as Jane wrestled it along the corridor the pan lid freed itself and the stale contents gushed forth covering her from platinum hair to shiny shoes. The stench was immediate and overwhelming.

The offending makeshift toilet was cast aside as Jane ran from the flat throwing her arms in the air whilst screaming expletives towards the discarded object. The scene in the front room remained unchanged the mourners seemed unimpressed by Jane's closing act. As she made a hasty exit, she brushed past me and the stretcher bearers, who were now doubled over with laughter. I chased after Jane and found her sitting in the passenger seat of the police vehicle in a state of shock, alternating between laughter, tears and gipping. I attempted to assure her that it was not too bad, only to be met with a barrage of abuse and an order to get driving, and I wasn't about to argue.

As if to join in the commotion, the rain was now bouncing down but that was never going to stop Jane and I from opening our respective windows and putting our heads out to take a soaking as we gasped for fresh air.

I have often wondered since how the sight of a speeding police car with two coppers hanging out of opposing windows in the pouring rain must have appeared to the numerous people we passed as we made our way back to the station.

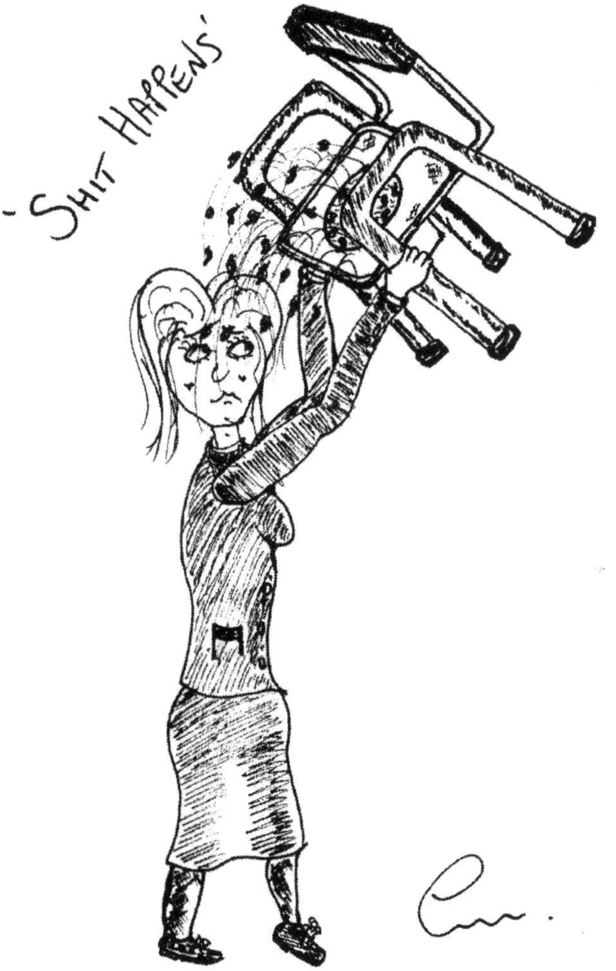
'SHIT HAPPENS'

18

Miners' Strike 1984-85

It was undoubtedly one of the most significant events in modern British history and I was there. This is how I saw it.

A short time after completing my two year probationary period I applied to be considered for the Divisional PSU (Police Support Unit), a relatively modern addition to policing. These units were introduced largely due to experiences gained from the football hooligans of the 1970s and the riots in Northern Ireland. The Police authorities had wisely decided to form a team of specially trained and equipped officers who could be quickly assembled and deployed for future large scale disturbances. This would prove to be a key factor in the forthcoming miners' strike.

Having been successfully inducted into the PSU, monthly training sessions were carried out at the Divisional HQ in Wakefield. Here we would spend hours running around in our fire resistant boiler suits, knee length steel toe capped leather boots and motorcycle style helmets complete with retractable perspex visors, carrying either a short or long perspex shield. All excellent forms of protection but for those who are able to remember the stifling heat of those 1980s summers, it's a miracle we didn't crumble with heat stroke and dehydration.

As a part of our training we would have to deal with groups of training staff playing the part of football hooligans or demonstrators, throwing bricks and bottles into our path together with the occasional petrol bomb, which would shatter across the transparent perspex shields showering flames over the on rushing rookies. Despite the fact we new these were nothing more than controlled exercises, the fire, bricks and bottles were real enough and the first hand experience would prove invaluable in the coming months.

The events of those twelve months between 5th March 1984 and 3rd March 1985 are as hotly debated today as they were over 30 years ago when the then Prime Minister, Margeret Thatcher, and Arthur Scargill, the Miners' Union President, first locked horns.

What I hadn't realised was how much time would be spent in the back of Transit vans with nine other hairy-arsed coppers sitting snugly on improvised wooden benches with next-to-no padding, fixed to the floor at opposite sides of the van and running the length of the rear of the van. Sleeping arrangements were anything but ideal and often two rows of six fully dressed men in blue would attempt to grab some sleep by leaning against the back of the adjacent man forming a human row of dominoes only prevented from toppling over by the end man being crushed against the plywood bulkhead separating our quarters from the driver's cab or 'Royal suite' as we called it. The Royal suite was home to our unit's CO, which in this case was our Divisional Inspector and his right hand man, the driver.

Cops are no different to anyone else and hour upon hour in a cramped van parked on a motorway service station car park, deserted country lane or disused military barracks would inevitably test the patience of the occupants. I guess that, in a strange way, this contributed to the bonding between an already close knit group of blokes who knew only too well the importance of watching each other's backs whenever we were deployed. We would while away the hours on standby doing the usual things, telling stories or jokes, reading and a considerable amount of singing. This included composing our own station anthem, which followed the tune from the Country Life butter advert of 1981 ('Can't get a better bit of butter on your knife').

'We are the lads from Laisterdyke.

You can't get a better bit of dork up your wife.

If she's got a big box and keeps it clean,

we'll fuck your wife in the morning.'

It was never long before the packs of playing cards appeared. A van favourite was three card brag. For a £1 stake a player stood the chance to win over a tenner. Not exactly on a par with the Vegas high rollers but a good little earner back in the 80s. Winning or not, it was a small price to pay for whiling away hours of otherwise mind numbing down time. These were only our van rules, and I witnessed many less friendly card schools when on standby in a school gym or other large holding area. On these occasions there could be as many as five hundred officers from several different force areas gathered under one roof and at times it seemed the only common ground we shared was the uniform we were wearing.

Poker was the game of choice for many and it wasn't uncommon to see vast amounts of money stacked on the makeshift gaming tables. Almost inevitably, it rarely took long for the already tired and stressed individuals to let fly with accusations of cheating, which would often lead to scuffles breaking out throughout the long tense afternoons. Still, at least this gave the onlookers an opportunity to rehearse their crowd control techniques. In an effort to let off some of this pent-up energy, games of football were often arranged where any spare grassland would suffice as a pitch and police helmets would take the place of goal posts. More pre match scuffles would take place as grown men would argue like school kids as to who would be on which team and play in which positions, etc.

The matches themselves were anything but friendly and were played with the ferocity of a local Yorkshire derby. A particular example occurred when one lad went in for a 50-50 challenge for the ball and came off second best receiving a double compound fracture of the shin as a reward.

So this would be our lifestyle for the next twelve months whilst we awaited deployment. Our record for consecutive days in captivity was twenty three.

Though the strikes were nationwide, many of the pits I attended were located in West Yorkshire, South Yorkshire and Nottinghamshire. The pit sizes varied as did the number of pickets. On occasion we would turn up mob handed expecting a big turn out only to find a handful of men and women holding placards by the pit entrance, as so called 'flying pickets' had been dispatched to other sites to call our bluff. There was always one constant, which was the frosty welcome we would receive as we rolled in and started moving people on. I guess the vast majority of strikers saw us as the enemy just doing Thatchers dirty work. I can see their point of view and they're entitled to it. For us, we had a job to do which was to ensure that those miners or 'scabs' as their colleagues labelled them, were able to enter their place of work without fear of physical harm. In addition we had to make sure that wagons were able to enter and leave the pits without damage or delay. I respected that these men and woman were doing what they thought was right to protect their livelihoods, but the level of violence displayed at some of the sites could never have been condoned or ignored.

In general, there would be a repeating pattern at most of the pits. The pickets would be gathered close to the colliery entrance, complete with banners and well rehearsed chants. We would form a blue line between the demonstrators and the road leading to the pit. Wagons would arrive to collect coal, or vehicles carrying the wanna-be workers (often hidden in the car boot, such was the fear of retribution should they be identified) and wagons leaving the yard filled with coal were the catalyst for increased aggression from the picketers. They would push forward to block their intended progress and we would link arms and push back to prevent the roads from being blocked. A few minutes of to-ing and fro-ing and things would settle down until the next arrival or departure. And so it would continue throughout the day.

There would generally be a half time break where both sides would be relieved for a lunch break. The team sergeant would usher us to a piece of spare ground away from the action and dish out the doggy bags containing a sandwich, chocolate bar, piece of fruit and a juice drink. Highlight of the day! Just like on the old school trips. A bit of swapping would take place: orange for a banana, tuna butty for a ham and tomato and so on. On occasions, once the food was scoffed, a group of miners would venture across with a football or cricket set and a game would take place, all differences forgotten. Then at the sound of an approaching vehicle all the players would sprint back to their respective sides of the battle lines and resume were they left off. They were the good days. Sadly, it wasn't always as amicable.

I remember being at one pit when we were particularly short of numbers. We took our positions as we normally did, a thin blue line facing a picket line four men deep and stretching hundreds of yards in either direction, with our backs to the road. This day had an electric feel right from the get go and as the first wagons began to arrive, the strikers upped the anti and made a hugh push towards the vehicles. We instinctively linked arms to strengthen our line but something had gone wrong. Some ten yards from our position two or three officers had been pulled forward off their feet into the crowd where they were taking a beating. Against instructions, four of us broke away from the line and ran over to the stricken men, leaving other officers to close ranks and reconnect the line.

As we reached the melee I could see the lads on the floor were getting a good hiding whilst being dragged futher into the baying crowd. Without time to assess things we jumped in to even things up. Plenty of blows were given and received but the objective was achieved and our fallen colleagues were located and dragged to safety, where they were treated for some minor injuries. To this day I'm not sure how we pulled it off without someone being seriously injured. Not much thought went into it, just instinct and adrenalin.

Later during our down time we were summonsed by our team Inspector who tore a strip from each of us for committing the cardinal sin of breaking the line. But with a wry smile on his face he redressed the balance by telling us it was the bravest thing he had seen since the troubles had started.

Orgreave Coking Plant

(The Main Event)

18th June 1984

On the eve of one of the biggest events in modern British history, we were transported overnight to awake and find ourselves parked amidst several rows of other divisional vans from numerous different force areas. There were vans of all shapes, sizes and colours, a good number of which looked like they hadn't seen the light of day in years let alone an MOT certificate. Some units had even travelled in rental vans. It was early morning and already there was an overwhelming feeling of anticipation and adrenalin circulating through the constantly swelling ranks of officers as they de-boarded their respective vans.

Unlike some of the less than friendly card schools and footy games when we had previously assembled, this time there was an unmistakable feeling of total camaraderie and solidarity. The holding area continued to fill as more vans arrived and parked up allowing the occupants to alight, stretch their legs and mingle with the rest of the gathering, exchanging thoughts as to what the day had in store.

Before too long Commanding Officers and Divisional Team Leaders were called to a briefing addressed by the highest ranking officers from the neighbouring forces. We had by now established that we were assembled in a small village close to Rotherham in South Yorkshire, a short drive from the Orgreave Coking Plant, a jewel in the miners' crown and maybe a last bastian of the Miners' Union. As with any large gathering, expectation and speculation was running wild through the ranks as they exchanged information and experiences from recent confrontations.

An hour or so after attending the briefing, our team leader returned to the unit and with a sombre tone began to address the parade with the details of our forthcoming engagement. In an instant the atmosphere around the camp had changed from loud and heady to silent and tense. This was to be by far the biggest show of strength and defiance by Scargill and his union members and we were told to prepare ourselves to face as many as 10,000 strikers, swelled by large numbers of known football hooligans and flying pickets drafted in from across the country. The reasoning behind this spectacular sized protest was in keeping with previous demonstrations but in addition, it was to create unprecedented news headlines.

As a police operational unit, we had amassed our largest assembly of officers to date numbering around 6,000, putting our numbers at around 60% of the protesters. We were informed that a relatively small police presence was in place at the Orgreave site. These officers were not trained in large scale disorder and were not equipped with protective clothing or equipment. Early reports of casualties had already been received and the thin blue line attempting to contain the situation and prevent the protesters from attacking the wagons as they entered the complex, were being forced to surrender ground.

Each unit at the holding area was given its own briefing and commands. Our deployment was straightforward: get to the centre of the flash point and relieve the lads on the front line.

Without hesitation we boarded our van and began the fifteen minute journey to our destination, using the travelling time to climb into our dark blue boiler suits and fasten the laces on our toe teckter boots.

We were brought to a halt in yet another designated holding area, this time less than a quarter of a mile from Orgreave Coking Plant. As the rear doors of the van were thrown open and we stepped out, the noise was instantly loud and unnerving. It wasn't like the organised chants at a football match but more like a concoction of random expletives and hate-filled threats.

As my eyes blinked through the bright sunlight I began to focus on what lay ahead. I had been present at countless football riots and large scale demonstrations but the scene here was a different level. As I stared in the direction of the pit I was grabbed by the overall picture. Mass upon mass of striking miners, hundreds deep and stretching both left and right as far as the eye could see. The giant silhouette of the pit building dominated the skyline and formed the awe inspiring backdrop to the swarming mass of bodies which moved relentlessly towards the comically thin blue line. It was like Custers' last stand.

There was no way the line of men should be holding together in the face of such force and it was certain it wouldn't hold for long. It was our time now. We made final equipment checks and donned our riot helmets, which had a strangely reassuring effect of dimming the sounds of the carnage which we were about to enter. As we lined up alongside the police van, each of my unit was handed a short perspex, transparent shield, as were other units stretching to my right and left. Our brief was to follow closely behind the units carrying the tall shields. Their objective was to relieve the officers currently on the front line and form a solid line of defence against the bricks and bottles which were already being thrown.

An order from our CO and we were en route to the front line at double quick time. This inevitably became a jog the closer we got to the action. Our wooden truncheons beating out a defiant rhythm against our head high shields. As we jogged forwards, we passed the horse mounted units to our left, whilst on our right, looking bruised, blooded and exhausted were the lads who had just been relieved from the heart of the action. Spontaneously, these same lads began clapping, cheering and fist pumping as they roared us onward like gladiators. Wow! It sent shivers down my spine and washed away any remaining trepidation. We're coming ready or not.

We jogged to a halt some five yards behind the tall shields and were given a thumbs up and a nod of approval from our Unit Inspector, like a proud father to his offspring, as he made his final pass along the line. Instantly, the volume was cranked up as more bricks, rocks and bottles were thrown our way over the top of the tall shields towards anyone unlucky enough to be caught in their line of flight. Within seconds, two officers within my eye line were felled by the flying objects and the previously straight line of short shields began to move forwards at random. A tap on the shoulder of the officer ahead and the long shields were swung inwards towards the charging short shields and just like that I was inside the dragons mouth reaching out to apprehend those identified as missile throwers.

This deployment was probably as dangerous as any we would undertake as once we crossed through the tall shields, they were closed behind us and we were completely isolated and open to attack from the incensed demonstrators as they fought remorselessly to prevent their comrades from being arrested. These snatches had to be made as quickly as possible and the targets removed to secure areas without delay. This pattern continued for what felt like the longest day, with surges and missile throwing followed by police snatch squads, interspersed with short periods of relative calm when chanting took centre stage, only to reignite into violence whenever a wagon was seen attempting to enter or leave the pit.

This was by no means the end of the miners' strike but nothing close to the scale of this event would occur again before the strike was officially ended in March 1985.

We continued to be deployed at various pits until the conclusion of the strike with the majority of demonstrations following the same pattern as those prior to Orgreave. There were, however, two notable events which occurred post-Orgreave whilst still deployed with the PSU.

Nostell Priory Music Festival

August 27th 1984

It remained a strange and frustrating atmosphere whenever we were herded into holding areas awaiting deployment to one of the pits. The period leading to Nostell had been one of the lengthiest periods of inactivity and the tension was culpable.

We had been placed on standby several times with a view to responding to pit disturbances but on each occasion, we had been stood down as surplus to requirements. Understandably, each time we had readied ourselves for action only for it to be cancelled, stress in the ranks had increased. During this particular period of down time, the whispers started to circulate round the lads. The annual music festival at Nostell Priory near to Wakefield, West Yorkshire was in full swing and organisers were concerned with the behavior of a section of those camping within the grounds of the event. As with most music festivals those attending came from all walks of life, the majority of which were there to have fun and enjoy the bands.

On this occasion the concern related to a large number of caravan dwelling travellers who, with no regard to anyone else, had used their forty or fifty caravans to form a camp within a camp. Undercover officers working inside the travellers' camp had obtained information that large quantities of illegal drugs were being sold and distributed from their temporary digs. No major surprise there I hear you say! It's a music festival! In addition it was believed that the drug dealers were in possession of shotguns and other life-threatening offensive weapons and as a result the alarm was raised.

So that was it; we were moving. Together with several other riot units, we travelled overnight from our holding area in South Yorkshire to the very edge of Nostell Priory. I chuckle when I recall this incident because the briefing was to search for and recover illegal substances and weapons and arrest those in possession. However, our parting instruction was to keep things as low key as possible. How was that a likely outcome? One hundred stressed-out coppers and more than four hundred armed drug dealers desperate to avoid arrest. Haha, you couldn't write this. Oh, I am doing!

Anyway, briefing over and we were buzzing at being given the lead role. Our Transit van set off over the crest and started to drop down into the valley housing the target camp, with our ten man unit following on foot at double quick time. For this operation we were wearing standard uniform and helmets, leather gloves on, and truncheons drawn.

We had hardly progressed ten yards when our van lurched to the right and smashed into the front of the first of the travellers' vans, which was attempting to exit the field at speed. That was that! Softly, softly out the window!

Our unit, together with several other units, began running down the hill towards the travellers', a number of which had already started to up-sticks and move out. As we ran down the hill, several of their vans were driving up the hill towards us, desperate to avoid capture.

It was every man for himself at this point, as we dodged the oncoming vehicles to reach the centre of the camp. It's difficult to know if the caravan dwellers were unable to hear us knocking on their doors, maybe as a result of prolonged exposure to excessively loud music, or that they were just not receptive to visitors that day. In either event, we were going in, ready-or-not. Caravan doors were pulled from their hinges as three, four and more coppers piled into the tiny interiors. Any occupants were either arrested for obstruction or placed to one side while cupboards and drawers, locked or otherwise, were opened and thoroughly searched for drugs and weapons. It seemed there were coppers and travellers fighting everywhere as the travellers attempted to dispose of evidence and resist arrest.

I recall that as I was entering one caravan, the door of the neighbouring van flew open and a huge guy in a string vest leapt into view waving a large meat cleaver towards the face of his unwelcome visitor. It never landed because a well-aimed truncheon struck the side of his head and he crumpled like a pack of cards.

The whole operation lasted about one hour and concluded with dozens of arrests, mainly for drugs, weapons and assault. A number of offensive weapons were recovered, including one of the alleged shotguns, a sword, knives, a hefty knuckle duster and countless other weapons whose original purpose was for the preparation of food, all of which were seized together with a good quantity of illegal substances.

Extreme Force

30th November 1984 Rhymney, South Wales

During the twelve month strike, a number of people lost their lives under different circumstances most notably David Wilkie, a thirty five year old taxi driver from South Wales. Mr Wilkie had, throughout the strike, ferried working miners to their place of work, enduring daily threats and abuse for his troubles. The tragedy occurred on 30th November 1984 as Mr Wilkie was driving his taxi along the A465 near Rhymney, Wales, conveying a so-called scab to their pit. As the vehicle he was driving approached a bridge, two striking miners threw a large concrete block from the top of the bridge through the windscreen of his car killing him instantly. The two striking miners were arrested and later convicted of murder and sentenced to life imprisonment. However, this sentence was subsequently reduced to manslaughter on appeal, largely influenced by pressure applied by the masses of striking miners who supported their colleagues. As a result, the two men served less than five years in prison.

Though I had no involvement in this incident, I have included it to highlight the extremes that certain people considered acceptable in order to further their cause.

Burgler Billy and the broken fag

I was looking forward to tonight's shift. For a few weeks now I had been working on a pattern of repeat burglaries occurring in the oversized council estate and a consistent MO (Modus Operandi) was becoming clear. The perpetrators were gaining entry to their chosen properties by a simple means of banging the palms of their hands against the metal window frame to spring open the window. Once inside, their first action was to slide a heavy piece of furniture up against the internal door, giving themselves extra time to escape back through the original entry point should the occupants be disturbed. Electrical items such as VCRs (video recorders), portable TVs and radios (this was the 80s) were the preferred booty along with cash and jewellery.

According to witness accounts, the majority of break-ins had occurred between midnight and 3am. The suspects were described as two afro-Caribbean males between five foot ten and six foot tall of stocky build and in their early twenties.

As a result of my efforts, I had persuaded my supervisors to allow me to put together a team of four officers to patrol the target areas during the relevant times, whilst wearing civilian clothing.

Game on! We split into two teams of two. I took 'Wobbly Gob' and having chosen one area to roam, team two headed off a few blocks in the opposite direction.

We began our tour around midnight and a heavy covering of snow looked like it could be as much a help as a hindrance. Tracks would be easier to follow and the bright white covering was illuminating the area like a floodlit stadium.

We had trudged through the snow for a couple of hours without really seeing or hearing anything aside from the statutory drunks staggering their way home. As 2am came and went the streets became very deserted, so much so that the crunching of snow beneath our boots would echo down the streets and we made the decision to turn off our police radios.

Just as we were starting to think this may not be our night, bingo! There they were. Two black lads matching the suspect's descriptions to a tee, were approaching us from the road to our left some thirty or forty yards away. They were casually walking along and chatting to each other, seemingly without a care in the world. This was made all the more staggering as one of the lads was clearly carrying a video recorder, whilst the second was also carrying a large electrical item. They did not appear at all concerned at our presence (thumbs up for our disguises) so we continued across the junction with their road until we were out of sight.

We ducked down behind a garden wall, waiting for them to come into view. It was perfect. In the next couple of minutes they would appear literally two yards from our grasp. As their voices got within striking distance Wobbly Gob had inexplicably chosen to turn his police radio back on and right on cue a message boomed out loud enough to wake the whole estate.

Shit! The stolen items were thrown into the night sky and the suspects took off at pace in opposite directions. I legged after the lad who had been carrying the recorder whilst Wobbly chased after the second man. My guy was quick like a bloody gazelle. This wasn't going to be easy. He shot off down a couple of narrow streets with me trying to keep pace some twenty or thirty yards adrift, when I saw him dive through an entrance door into a block of flats.

Within seconds I was inside the block via the same door. Nothing. Damn, he could be anywhere. Then 'bang.' The communal door at the far side of the building slammed shut. I charged out through the rear door and back into the estate. Which way? Result! The snow covering had indeed been kind and the fresh foot prints took off to the right and sure enough there he was, still sprinting away towards a second block of flats, again in through the front door and straight out of the rear.

Now at this point I wasn't really losing any ground but I sure as hell wasn't gaining any. He continued like a hare on speed, down one street up another, over a wall, then a garden fence back into the main estate. I was blowing now, always a sprinter never a marathon man. If this goes much further, I'm done. Much to my relief as I looked up he began to slow. He wasn't up for the marathon either. I continued to jog towards him as he came to a halt. As I drew level with him he turned to face me with his hands in the air, "I'm done man, you got me" he shouted. My lungs were hanging out and I could hardly muster a response, so I took hold of his arm and ushered him across the road, to the nearby pavement. "I'm good man, I ain't going anywhere" he informed me. Sweet music to my ears for sure as I wasn't going anywhere in a hurry either.

We made use of a street sign to take the weight off our legs and he asked if I had any smokes. I reached into my jacket and produced a crumpled packet. Looking into the pack it was clear all the filters had been snapped from the remaining fags. "Sorry pal, we're out of luck" He must have seen the look of despair on my face as he reached across and took the packet from my hand. "No worries man. I'll show you a trick." Then, with all the skill and dexterity of a surgeon, he took one of the separated tips and tapped out the loose flakes of baccy which left a small collar of paper into which he twisted one of the cigarette shafts. He handed me the finished article then performed the same operation on a second cig. Just for the briefest of moments we had a strange bonding as we talked and smoked our cigarettes. The divisional van arrived and Billy Boy was hauled off to the Bridewell.

During interview later that day he confessed to over 200 offences including car theft and burglaries, for which he received a lengthy custodial prison sentence.

20

Football Crazies

Football grounds in the eighties were often very violent places, continuing on from the craze started by the skinhead gangs of the previous decade. Public disorder and violence at football matches throughout the country became the norm.

Being a big fan of football, if I wasn't already allocated football duties, I would volunteer. The overtime was handy and more often than not, I would get to see some of the game.

Due to my location, the majority of games I would attend would be at Valley Parade, the home ground of Bradford City, but on occasion we might be deployed to other local grounds such as Elland Road, home of Leeds United, or Leeds Road Stadium, Huddersfield Town (replaced by the Alfred McAlpine Stadium in 1994) or a number of other, smaller grounds local to the area

It was inevitable that I would encounter some if not all of the notorious hooligan crews of the era, including the six worst crews as listed by the Six O' Clock News in 1985.

Bradford City – Ointment

Leeds United – Service Crew

West Ham – Inter City Firm

Millwall – Bushwackers

Blackpool – Rammy Arms Crew

Reading – Berkshire Boot Boys

Arsenal – The Herd

Along with many others such as:

Manchester United – Red Army

Chelsea – Headhunters

All of which had large contingents, many of which would travel to away games not for the football but for the fighting.

It seems strange now as I look back because few of the hundreds of games I attended resulted in major incidents. Maybe that mindset is a result of repetitiveness and acceptance/inevitability that large scale disturbance and fighting occurred almost every weekend and only the most extreme events would stand out.

On reflection, each and every one of the games I attended would require major planning and coordination and had their own inherent dangers.

Rather than going into great detail about each and every game I attended and risk sounding repetitive, because the reality is that most of the games followed a very similar pattern: fighting on the way to the ground, fighting inside the ground and yet more fighting on route for the train home. I thought I would just throw in some highlights of a few incidents I can recall, some humorous others harrowing, all typical of most games occurring up and down the country during the 80s.

Darts

Not the pop band of the same era but the common darts thrown in every boozer on a Friday night. Weapons of every description such as stanley knives, hammers, machetes even firearms have been involved with football hooligans but for me one of the scariest weapons was the dart, because chances were you would never see or hear it coming. My first experience with the dart being used as a weapon came at a game where Huddersfield were hosting the Millwall and their notorious Bushwacker crew. I was placed with the home fans in the cop end of the ground alongside a metal chain link fence designed to keep the opposing fans apart. The fence was to a large degree successful in its purpose, in that despite the fans being very close, physical contact was not really possible. It did of course allow them to see each other and exchange pleasantries but to a large extent that was all.

That was until a number of the away fans armed themselves with darts, which they managed to get past the turnstile searches when entering the ground. It was during the second half of an otherwise forgettable afternoon that I remember catching sight of around a dozen darts flying through the air from the Bushwacker section into the unsuspecting Huddersfield fans. I don't now how many darts hit their targets, and I can't recall there being any serious injuries, but I do remember the young lad standing by my side turning to me with a look of shock and horror on his face as he pointed to his arm who asked me if I would remove the dart that was buried in his shoulder. He lived to tell the tale, which I'm sure he did, many times with varying degrees of embellishment. Fair play, he probably earned that.

Flying Helmet

I rarely policed the Huddersfield games but in 1986 I was there again, chuffed to be drafted in as part of the extra policing for the visit of the mighty Arsenal FC. It was the league cup 2nd round 2nd leg and a full house was anticipated.

As it turned out I was positioned at the very top of the Huddersfield Kop and I was unable to see anything of the pitch. The kop was packed to the rafters and it was almost impossible to raise a hand from my side, not ideal if it kicked off. That said the atmosphere was generally good natured albeit high spirited.

My partner for the match was my buddy Wobbly Gob who was standing some 20 yards to my left, though I was unable see him. The first half came and went without incident, just the usual shouting, chanting and singing. It wasn't to last, as part way into the second half I saw a police helmet flying into the air away to my left, exactly where Wobbly would have been standing. '

"The copper's lost his head, the copper's lost his head. Ee ey addy oh the copper's lost his head." Rang out around the Kop. "Oh shit!" I couldn't reach my radio so started to push my way through the dense crowd. Not dense as in stupid, dense as in ….. Oh never mind.

The fans weren't making my journey easy and in the few minutes it took to reach my pal he had not only lost his helmet, but his jacket and clip on tie had also gone walk about. Wobbly was fine albeit a bit shocked and embarrassed, God knows what state of undress he would have been in if it had taken me any longer to reach him.

Those responsible for the striptease were long gone, shepherded away by their allies, who took great delight in cheering and applauding as I ushered Wobbly out of the Kop and down to the sanctuary of the holding area.

Headhunters

In the late 80s in the old division 2, the Chelsea Headhunters travelled to their hosts Bradford by train, smashing up the carriages and fighting with staff and terrorising other passengers en route. A number of officers, including myself, were dispatched to the train station located in Bradford town centre, together with a number of dog units, to greet the oncoming hooligans.

It could be argued that there is no such thing as a good place to have a scrap but a train station platform is definitely not recommended.

To spice up the tension, we had been briefed a couple of hours earlier by the commanding officer. Pre-match briefings were standard practice but what made this one different was the information that members of the Headhunters were carrying Stanley knives and blades concealed inside their jacket linings and in particular we were to look for gang members wearing long leather coats as these were the generals (as they chose to call themselves).

On arrival at the Bradford Interchange train station, the Transport Police had done a good job of clearing the immediate area. The information was that there were approximately 100 Headhunters on the train, which gave them a slight advantage in numbers and also meant that things were going to get pretty cramped. The rumbling sound travelling along the tracks gave us a heads up that the train was approaching. Chin straps down and gloves on. Here we go!

As the train came to a halt we had to run in units of ten to an allocated carriage door. The chanting could already be heard through the open windows. Nothing friendly here. No, these were chants of violence, unsurprisingly directed towards the boys in blue who were there to spoil their away day plans.

As the doors separated, the intoxicated travellers flooded out onto the paved area alongside. The air was electric enough to have run the trains if they hadn't been diesel. There was lots of pushing and shoving as the chanting was now enhanced with raised arms waving the insults our way. We created make-shift search areas and looked for the most likely candidates to pat down for concealed weapons. Unsurprisingly, this didn't go down well and when a shout went out from within their ranks that they were getting turned round and sent home on the next train, all hell broke loose.

There were punches being thrown from every direction. The noise was deafening albeit incoherent. Bodies on both sides were knocked to the ground and when one of their crew started to wade in with a boot into the ribs of a stricken copper, I leapt forward and with an arm around his neck, pulled him backwards. But before I could complete the manoeuvre, I felt a fist crash against my ear and down I went. This was not the place to be as there were boots (trainers) flying everywhere. Then, as quickly as I had hit the deck, I quite literally had my collar felt as I was pulled back onto my feet, my ear pulsing like a Belisha beacon and ringing like an alarm bell.

"Move!" I did, just in time as a half full beer can smashed into the helmet of the copper behind me, knocking it from his head and showering him with the contents. No real harm done just a criminal waste of good beer.

A number of the hooligans had already been wrestled to the ground and cuffed allowing the dog handlers to move in with their pets and gently manoeuvre the ringleaders up against a wall. This coincided neatly with the arrival of police backup units who promptly marched those who had previously entertained the dogs across to the far side of the train station where a special train waited to convey them back to the smoke. A good number had managed to get away during the fighting and had used the railway tracks as an unlikely means of escape. Most if not all where subsequently rounded up and sent packing with their predecessors.

Zulu Dawn

In the mid 80s it was the turn of the Birmingham City Zulus to visit Valley Parade. This was a another crew with a violent reputation and this day would do nothing to dispel those claims. My roll was to patrol the away fans entrances into the ground, and I was pleased to be in the company of a large number of other police officers including a couple of dozen horse mounted bobbies and a handy contingent of dog handlers. As kick off approached, reports of fighting in and around the town had been broadcast through the police radios and tensions were rising.

A large number of the Birmingham fans had still not made it inside the ground due to the thorough searches taking place at the turnstiles and it's likely that word of the isolated Brummies had circulated to members of the Bradford Ointment as a hundred or so came running into view from either side of the stadium effectively ambushing the Zulus. It erupted into a mass battle, with bodies running in every direction, some trying to reach safety others to join in the fights which were taking place everywhere.

The mounties were quick to respond charging their steeds and wielding their batons towards the rioters. Now this was always an effective way of breaking up large scale disorder, however the horses were no great respecters of sex, creed or colour and that included blue uniforms. So it was generally a good idea to let them have their fun before getting to close.

One dog handler however found himself caught up in the melee with his trusted mutt straining at the leash. In an act of the utmost bravery or total stupidity, one of the Zulu crew felt compelled to run at the snarling dog and take a kick at its face. Initially he must have been elated as the dog let out a loud yelp and staggered to the side dazed by the blow.

What this idiot hadn't taken into account was just how attached the handlers are to their pets. In a split second the dog handler had leapt through the air in a Kung Fu style move and landed a pin point kick of his own right into this guy's bollocks. Down he went, writhing in agony and screaming like a baby. This didn't seem to appease the handler who obviously felt more corporal punishment was required as he proceeded to leap onto the stricken Zulu.

This was my cue and I took hold of the injured party dragging him away and arresting him for his own safety as much as for the breach of the peace. Sadly for me, this meant I would have no further involvement in the game. But hey, at least my jewels were intact.

Beat the Drum

On occasions even the best laid plans don't go according to plan.

It was a rare away day for me to be at Elland Road where Leeds United were playing host to Ipswich Town in the old league division one. For reasons I was never privy to hundreds of extra officers had been drafted in for this fixture. Maybe it was nothing more than the reputation of the Leeds Service crew or perhaps information had been received which suggested something big was going down. Whatever the reason, there were literally hundreds of coppers on duty including mounted officers and dog handlers. The crowd attendance would be a little over 20,000. I along with a dozen or so other bobbies drew the short straw for this one, carpark duty before, during and after the match.

The fans arrived at the ground seemingly in good spirits and entered the stadium with the minimum of fuss. Now all I had to do was kill the next 90 minutes wandering around the huge carpark, which was devoid of people. It was a cold February afternoon so me and the other lads took turns between having a patrol around the area followed by a fifteen minute warm up onboard one of the many coaches that were still attended by their respective drivers.

It was on one of my coach breaks that the chink in this match's master plan revealed itself. The match commanders had taken the gamble of drafting in any available officers from the neighbouring towns, effectively placing all their eggs in one basket, consciously leaving those areas under manned. This decision would have seemed fully justifiable at the time it was made, as there didn't appear to be any other high risk events taking place within the force area.

As I listened to a sports channel on the coach radio, confirmation of the commander's oversight came through the speakers loud and clear. The half-time goals round up was interrupted by the live commentary of a very excited reporter at the Shay Stadium in Halifax. He relayed his disgust at the behaviour of several hundred Blackpool 'Muckers' who had travelled from Lancashire across the Pennines to watch their team take on fourth division Yorkshire rivals Halifax Town. The trouble had erupted at the end of the first half when seats were ripped from the away supporters stand and hurled onto the pitch. The 'Muckers' had then run onto the playing surface and made a be-line for the marching band, knocking the bass drummer to the ground and stamping holes into the skin of the drum before charging on to confront the Halifax fans.

Meanwhile back at Elland Road the game reached full time and the away fans were escorted to their coaches and the train station, with hardly a sign of trouble, the lack of agro almost certainly due to the huge police presence.

In sharp contrast, just 16 miles away at the Shay stadium in Halifax, the handful of coppers covering the game with Blackpool must have been run ragged as they tried in vain to contain the running battles throughout the afternoon.

Bradford City v Leeds United

Odsal Stadium Sept. 1986

The season following the Valley Parade fire disaster, Bradford's home games were relocated to alternative grounds whilst rebuilding work took place. A number of the games were played at neighbouring Leeds and Huddersfield but the majority were held at the Odsal Top Stadium, home of the Bradford Northern Rugby League Club (now the Bradford Bulls).

This created numerous policing headaches for the hierarchy. The ground itself had only two open stands with zero segregation. This was not an issue at the rugby matches where there was little if any crowd trouble. A couple of metal fences were erected inside the stands which acted as makeshift segregation between the opposing football fans. On the majority of occasions, however, away supporters would gather at the end of the ground that was little more than a huge grass bank, on which a number of large concrete steps had been laid forming very basic terracing at the foot of which a two foot tall brick wall stood between the fans and the pitch. The pitch itself was a good distance from the crowd due to a dirt track, used for speedway and stock cars, which ran around the perimeter. The biggest problem was the location of the ground. Bradford city centre is built at the base of a large valley, with Odsal stadium being some two miles away at Odsal Top. As almost all travelling fans would arrive in the city centre by train or coach it meant they had to be escorted on foot along Manchester Road, a duel carriage way carrying large volumes of traffic both in and out of the city. The journey along Manchester Road included a number of pubs and a large filling station complete with its own mini-market. In addition, the road was lined on both sides with a mix of industrial estates and private dwellings. Trying to contain even the smallest group of fans along this stretch of road was at best difficult. For those not wishing to be chaperoned, it was near impossible.

On this particular day, I was partnered up with my best pal Lightbulb. We had worked the footy together many times, had seen most things and been in a good few scraps together. Our directive was to patrol on foot approximately half way up Manchester Road close to one of the pubs that had become a hot spot for trouble. Our secondary objective was to monitor the crowds as they made their way out from the city and ensure that they didn't deviate from their route to the stadium.

The Bradford crew, the 'Ointment', had taken to using the long stretch of road, with its relatively limited police presence, to hide in the abundance of side roads and buildings until the away fans appeared at which point they would ambush them either in a close combat punch-up or with a shower of bricks and bottles.

We began our patrol a couple of hours or so before the scheduled kick-off about a mile up from the city centre. Other pairs of officers also patrolled different sections of the road. As we were generally unable to see our nearest allies, radio contact was essential and as a result a dedicated channel was allocated for use on football details, and the radios would remain on talk through. Anything said by any officer via his radio could be heard instantly by all the officers on that frequency. This eliminated the time normally lost relaying messages through the control room.

Always a bit of added spice for the local Derbies, and it would be no exaggeration to say that the Bradford 'Ointment' and the Leeds 'Service Crew' had a special hatred for each other. No one was doubting there would be violence. The only questions were when and to what degree.

As we entered the final hour before kick off, me and Lightbulb remarked to each other how quiet it had been. There had been little or no radio activity and we had only seen a handful of fans making their way to the ground. This was unusual to say the least as the average turn out for this fixture would be in the region of 13,000.

It was as though we had tempted the fates because right then the radios crackled and a voice notified us that there had been fighting in one of the city centre pubs. A number of arrests had been made but approximately 100 youths from both crews had run from the scene in the direction of Manchester Road towards the stadium. Within a couple of minutes the radio went again, "Fighting in lumps Manchester Road, up from the train station."

This time the sound of shouting and chanting could be heard surrounding the reporting officer.

It was kicking off! Now the adrenalin was starting to flow. We were too far away from this melee to get involved but it was a sure bet it would be heading our way. Sirens could be heard and blue lights were flashing as police vans and patrol cars raced from every direction to the given location. Just like that, everything came to life. There seemed to be groups of fans everywhere chanting their team songs and hurling the statutory abuse at anyone in a blue uniform as they made their way to the ground. It was important to let these numpties have their moment as we could ill afford to become involved with trivial matters when the real problem lay ahead.

As if to prove my point, the one call every copper dreads hearing blared out of the radio. "Ten thirteen. Ten thirteen. Filling station Manchester Road." This was a call that was NEVER used unless an officer's life was in immanent danger. Fuck! Instinctively, I set off running closely followed by Lightbulb. My adrenalin was through the roof and my heart was pumping like a steam train. The filling station was a good half a mile away and on the opposite side of the road. Lightbulb and I leapt into the city bound lane without really considering the risk and more by luck than judgement, we made it across the carriageway and over the central reservation and into the traffic making its way from the city centre.

Again we got lucky and made it across the road unscathed to the safety of the pavement. As we legged it down the hill towards the garage, coppers seemed to appear from everywhere. I had never imagined there were so many bobbys on duty at any one time. Flashing blue lights and sirens could be seen and heard as the mobile units approached at speed seemingly from every side street and junction. Some vehicles had only the driver on board where others had packed in so many occupants that the back end of the car was almost dragging on the floor.

I felt like I was running in treacle, maximum effort for minimal progress, yet a few minutes later I was there. It was breathtaking. Police vans and patrol cars were abandoned everywhere, on the forecourt, the main carriageway, pavements, grass verges literally everywhere. Hundreds of coppers where running in different directions. Some towards the filling station, others across to the opposite side of Manchester road where fights had broken out between the rival crews.

In one corner of the forecourt large numbers of hooligans had been contained by a ring of coppers. Rugby tackles and truncheons were flying as more fights broke out. This was not an organised rounding up of a few naughty boys: it was personal. One of ours had been seriously injured and these wankers were responsible. Injured bodies lay on the ground with cuts and bruising while others limped away to join their mates who had moved a few hundred yards away from the garage in the direction of the stadium.

As those who had been arrested were shipped off to the bridewell, ambulance staff continued to treat the officer to whom the 'ten thirteen' call related. Details started to filter through as to what had occurred. PC Graham, one of the good guys, was someone I knew well having spent many hours in his company during the miners' strike. He had responded to a call from the garage attendant regarding theft and damage. On his arrival he had been hit in the face with a house brick thrown by one of the hooligans. As he lay helpless on the floor a number of the same thugs had taken turns to kick him about the head and body, before running away. The call for assistance had been radioed in by his partner who had also received serious injuries including a broken wrist.

PC Graham remained unconscious as medical staff strapped him onto a stretcher before conveying him to the Bradford Royal Infirmary. Miraculously, within a few months PC Graham was fully recovered and back at work. All we knew at the time was that a friend and colleague was badly injured.

The atmosphere was electric. The Superintendent and commanding officer for this match day arrived at the scene and conducted an ad-hoc briefing for the gathering of coppers waiting for new instructions. As it turned out there weren't any. We were simply told to continue policing the match as per the original directive. Not hugely helpful in light of recent events, but it did at least give the lads a few minutes to catch their breath and regain some composure.

The kick-off was only minutes away and the streets were all but empty as the majority of fans were now inside the stadium. Lightbulb and I together with a few others were ferried to the ground in one of the vans and we too made our way into the main stand where the home fans were gathered.

These fixtures were always fiercely contested both on and off the pitch and the atmosphere inside this bowl shaped arena was buzzing. As the game got underway both sets of fans were already running through their respective repertoires of songs and chants, in the main derogatory and threatening ditties aimed at their oppos.

As was the norm, the away supporters (in this case Leeds United) were assembled on the sloping grass bank behind one of the goals. The first signs of trouble came twenty minutes into the first half when a number of the Leeds Service Crew climbed over the low concrete wall and ran across the cinder track towards the main stand. Members of the Bradford Ointment responded by charging towards the oncoming threat. I ran to the area where the two sets of rival crews were squaring up to each other, pulling people out of way in order to get to the front of the stand. Thirty or so other coppers quickly arrived and together we formed a make shift human barrier keeping the two crews apart as they continued to gesticulate and taunt each other.

As more bobbies reached the hot spot, a number of the ring leaders from both sides were either arrested for public order offences or escorted from the ground with the remainder being herded back onto the grass bank. More officers were subsequently deployed to the area which had the desired effect of preventing any similar confrontations.

That was until ten minutes from the end of the game. With Bradford leading 2-0 the 'Service Crew' had one more stunt to play, which was to set fire to a portable chip van adjacent to the grass bank. A mere sixteen months after the horrors of the Valley Parade fire, memories of the disaster were still very raw amongst many of the Bradford supporters. Some tried to reach the Leeds fans to vent their anger whilst others, fearing for their safety, tried to flee the stadium. With panic setting in around the ground I instinctively ran towards the grass verge, I had no real plan, I don't know if it was concern for the safety of fans near the burning van or a desire to take down the idiots who had started it. It was probably a bit of both, certainly the earlier incident with PC Graham was still fresh in my mind.

With most of the coppers inside the ground, now assembled by the foot of the grass bank and the fire brigade attempting to tackle the fire, the Leeds nutters stepped it up a level and started showering anyone from the emergency services, coppers and fire fighters, with lumps of concrete, bricks and bottles. That was the signal to go in.

Dodging the oncoming debris I made a bee line for one of the pricks who was readying himself to throw a lump of concrete. Smack! I nailed him with a peach of a right hook and he was down. The only problem I had now was that once you bagged yourself a prisoner you effectively took yourself out of the action. I didn't have to worry about that too much as it happened because, before I could get my cuffs on the twat, the entire Leeds contingent ran down from the terraces snatching their pal from my grip, as they swept past me, before charging across the pitch to the far side of the ground with the intention of fighting the Bradford fans. I might have lost that one but by the end of the afternoon collectively we had made 75 arrests and more would follow with the aid of CCTV.

21

No Place For a Kid

I found myself standing in the middle of the town centre mortuary. I couldn't recall exactly why I was there. I think it was to collect some court papers. In truth it doesn't really matter.

The Head Pathologist was occupied talking to three of his technicians, each dressed in their green operating gowns, some eight or nine yards in front of me. As a typical nosey copper I thought I would use the waiting time to take in the clinical surroundings. Immediately to my left three stainless steel examination/operation tables were laid alongside of each other forming a perfect row. Each table was immaculately clean and completely baron with the exception of the veed out rubber block waiting to support the neck of the next customer.

Beyond the tables, a continuous stainless steel work surface was fixed along the length of the wall, above which steel cupboards were fixed to complete the stainless set, all brightly illuminated beneath the specialist overhead lighting. I recalled how I and several other recruits had attended the mortuary to observe a number of autopsies as part of our induction training. The sights, smells and sounds of which were supposed to ready us for situations we would almost certainly encounter during our service. To a large degree the objective was achieved but nothing could have prepared me for what I would gaze upon as I turned my head.

There to my right, no more than a few feet away, were more examination tables creating a mirror image of the ones to my left. Only this time one of the tables was not empty. Curled up in a fetal position across the corner of the table closest to me was what looked like a perfectly formed baby, maybe a mere six weeks old. Instantly, the glare of the lights became even more intense as though I was under the spotlights on a stage. I felt numb and heady and in an effort to rationalize what lay before me I tried to convince myself this baby was infact nothing more than a working model, which would be used for training purposes. I so wanted that to be the case but I new this was the body of a tiny child.

I lifted my head and caught sight of the group of mortitions standing before me. They weren't talking any more. Now they were focused on me, their expressions confirming my worst fears yet offering me reassurance and even compassion. These incredible people have the ability and strength of mind to be able to deal with such sadness on an all too regular basis, yet I could see in their eyes that they knew, albeit I was a seasoned cop, this was a first and I was hurting. I turned again to face the little fella. He looked so perfect. Chubby cheeks and wrinkles, tiny little fingers and toes, even the milky pink colouring. Not a blemish. His eyes were shut and he looked so peaceful, curled up as though he was just sleeping, but at the same time he looked cold and lonely on his vast steel grey resting place, and I wanted to hold him.

My youngest son was a similar age at the time, and my heart was in bits. How must his parents have felt and how did they deal with the ultimate loss? Incomprehensible.

The image of this little boy remains with me now as though it were yesterday.

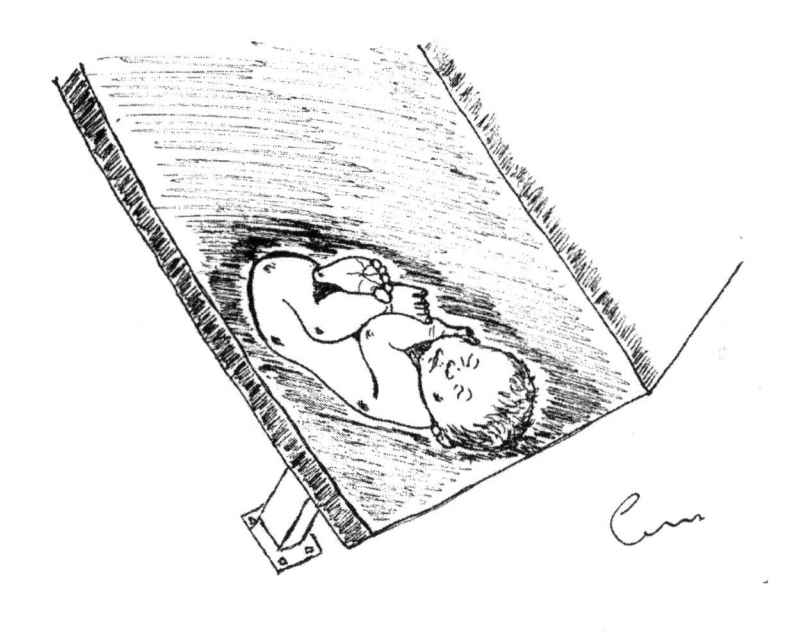

Sleep in peace little fella

Alone as you lay

For here in my heart

Forever you'll stay

(Extract from 'Ramblings of a broken man' Poetry by Tim Mills)

22

Treasure Hunt

The annual team outing was always great fun and often unpredictable. This particular year was to be no different. The destination was a campsite in the tranquil village of Hawes, North Yorkshire, a weekend of total relaxation away from the rigours of work related stresses.

Friday came and everything was packed. Well, the essentials: beer, wine a change of clothes and a second hand, one bedroomed tent. These trips were open to everyone from the shift including wives, husbands, girlfriends, boyfriends, sisters, brothers, friends, anyone. Me and the missus, Jan had just picked up a set of wheels in the shape of a ten year old Hillman Imp, finished in an eye catching faded pea green colour. 'Oh Wow!' I hear you say, 'you lucky bastard'. Well, I can tell you that owning such a thoroughbred did come with its draw backs. They were very tiny cars with a rear mounted engine and enough room in the boot, located at the front of the car, to store nothing more than a handbag. As a result, our tent had to be transported in my mate's car.

No worries. Nothing was going to spoil this trip. Was it? We're off, nice and early Friday morning-a lovely sunny day. We were soon out of the Bradford suburbs and into the beautiful surrounding countryside.

We had travelled for about an hour and twenty minutes and were no more than ten miles from our destination. This should have been where the treasure hunt began. The previous week one of the lads had left clues hidden along the route to the campsite to be collected for a friendly competition. Essentially who ever gathered the most clues and was able to decipher them correctly won a case of beer courtesy of the team kitty. The ultimate incentive to grab the attention of a group of beer swilling coppers. At least that's how it should have panned out.

Unfortunately, what I had not foreseen was just how badly my jalopy would handle the numerous steep inclines that led to the promised land. The first signs that all was not well came as we twisted our way up the first relatively tame incline. The temperature gauge rose quickly towards the overheating mark. "Don't worry" I assured Jan "She will be fine. We are nearly there now." "Shit" we had only travelled a short distance up the very next 2 in 1 gradient when the little buggy came to a grinding halt in the middle of the road, steam gushing from the rear.

As I stood at the side of my vehicle offering words of encouragement like "you fucking useless piece of crap, why me, why now, for fuck sake." I heard a gaggle of laughter behind me. I turned to see half a dozen of the gang wetting themselves at my current predicament. "That's it laugh it up, you wankers" I suggested, already starting to laugh myself as I began to see the funny side. Our laughter was short lived however as a queue of cars were quickly backing up behind us, with irate occupants sounding their horns, impatiently.

No worries, all hands on deck and with some major huffing and puffing from eight volunteers, the dead Hillman Imp was pushed into a lay-by some hundred yards further up the mountain. Having grabbed the beer and wine from the boot alternative transport was found in the back of Lightbulb's chariot and despite there being five of us on the back seat, we were on our way once more.

Lightbulb was my closest friend be it at work or leisure. He was a laugh a minute never taking life to seriously, and he was a bloody good copper.

After the cramped but thankfully short journey we were there. The field. Our home for the next two nights. This campsite was quite literally a field with no real facilities to speak of other than the bar. I call it a bar, in fact it was an old barn where beer was served. What more could these travelling coppers have wished for.

After an hour or so of hysterics watching everyone attempt to erect their tents, inside out, upside down, short pole where a long pole should go, etc, we were done. Finally, we could party. "Everyone to the bar, the barn, the bar. Whatever, let's get some beers in." No one needed a second invitation and it was every man for himself as we stampeded to the watering hole.

The interior was a reflection of the exterior, uncovered Yorkshire stone walls, periodically decorated with quality prints, such as the dogs playing pool. A long wooden bar top with two beer pumps occupied the rear of the large single lounge room. A dozen or so tables complete with chairs were dotted around in no real order. But there was a pool table with stitched up baize and most importantly, a dart board. We loved playing darts. As it turned out the darts had been stolen, but hey we were on holiday who needed 'sport'.

The drinks gatherers had already converged on the bar taking orders as they did so. The remainder dragged all available tables and chairs together to form a large communal area where everyone could talk to each other. The drinks began to flow, as is common practice for off duty coppers or on duty CID for that matter. As the drinks went down, so the volume of banter went up. It wasn't long before everyone found themselves listening to Lightbulb as he recited one of his recent outings.

"I had to go nick Ivor the other day. You know, the west Indian lad who's always selling drugs to the kids. Turns out his bird had dobbed him in after he gave her a black eye. I had to do a bit of digging to find where he was hiding out, but I got some info that he was bunked up with his mate in a flat inside the square.

I've brought him in before and he's not usually any bother but you never know, plus I didn't know who's flat he was in, so I took one of the probationers with me to introduce him so to speak. Anyway, we arrived at the flat one afternoon after being told he was definitely there. But, despite banging on the door for ten minutes, there was no answer. My side kick looked a little disappointed as he enquired if there was anything else we could do. "There's one other thing we could try. It's a long shot but you never know", I told him as I pushed open the letter box in the front door, shouting into the flat in my best Caribbean accent. "Hey Ivor, it's me Winston, man. What you doin'. I need to get in man."

The recruit's mouth fell open in shock. I'm not sure if it was a result of my unorthodox policing techniques or the fact that Ivor actually fell for it and opened the door. Still there wasn't time to find out because as soon as Ivor realised I wasn't his mate Winston, probably due to the blue uniform, he was off, down the steps to the car park outside. I gave chase closely followed by my bewildered rookie. I pushed open the door to the car park just in time to see Ivor starting to drive away in his car. As he drove past almost running us both over, I legged it up to the driver's window and using my police radio, which was already in my hand, I smashed the door glass, reached in through the opening and turned off the ignition. I am not sure who's face was the funniest, Ivor's or the new lads, but either way Ivor wasn't about to argue with this nut case copper as he obligingly slipped on the handcuffs and walked with me to the cop car".

Laughter rang out together with a few shouts of good job Lightbulb. Then Angie claimed next go.

"A few of us were on nights a few weeks back when most of you were skiving on the miners strike. We were on a real skeleton crew. Desk jockeys that hadn't seen the streets for years were having to take cars out just to make the numbers up. Anyway, the few of us that were on duty were single manned so obviously the instructions were not to put ourselves at unnecessary risk. (Laughter-like we had a choice). I think it was about two in the morning when a shout came over the radio. Officer in trouble. Gas bottle storage unit. Thornbury. I wasn't that far away so I stuck my blue light on and went for it. I can't tell a lie I was pretty pleased when a rapid response vehicle with its horns and lights going flew past me just before I got there. I thought "thank God I wont be the only one there." Angie briefly stopped talking to look across the table at Wobbly who had a bemused look on his face, before continuing. "I'm sorry Wobbly but I will never forget the sight that greeted me when I pulled up along side the gas unit. You were clinging onto that enormous traveller's back as he ran round the compound swinging you from side to side like you were a rag doll. But fair play, there was no way you were letting go and it turned out a bloody good collar because not only did he get nicked but we recovered a few hundred quid's worth of industrial gas bottles that he had loaded onto his wagon".

More laughter and a few sarcastic shouts of "way to go Wobbly," before Tony took his turn. It's worth mentioning that Tony was a big lad about 6' 2" tall, stocky build and he new how to look after himself.

He started "Anyone met a guy called 'Scouse Adams?" everyone looked blank so he continued. "No I hadn't either until the other day. I was on my own when I got a call to attend the 'Old Cul-de-sac' in Bierley. I didn't realise until then that the Ratfink family, you know the ones, bully by sheer weight of numbers, take the law into their own hands regardless, hard as nails, blah blah blah. Well, it turns out they occupy most of the 20 town houses on the one way in, one way out cul-de-sac. Anyway it turned out that they had met their match in the form of one guy, namely 'Scouse Adams' who in the words of the Ratfink family leader 'Old Man Ratfink' as he rang for police assistance, was using threatening behaviour towards them. I parked my car at the entrance to the cul-de-sac and started walking in.

A dozen or so of the Ratfinks were standing at their respective garden gates wielding baseball bats in the general direction of the centre of the cul-de-sac where the lone figure of what I can only describe as the human equivalent of a Silverback gorilla was pacing up and down. As I approached the Silverback, I could hear his ultimatum directed towards the Ratfinks. "If anyone of use wants to take a swing at me with those bats go ahead. But if you do, make sure you kill me cos if I get up I will shove them bats up your arses and turn you all into popsicles."

None of the Ratfinks seemed too keen on the kind offer and instead relinquished their title as hard men, choosing instead to call on their long term foe the 'copper' to get rid of the gorilla in their midst. (See what I did there!).

As I reached the gorilla, his true size was overwhelming. He was a good 6'8'' tall and was built like the original brick shit house. As he turned towards me, the face on his huge head showed the clear signs of a man who had lived a violent life. A nose that travelled in several directions, cauliflower ears and countless facial scars. I took a deep breath. "Ok, pal. What's the problem here?" I asked him. He grimaced, choosing not to answer my question and stared straight through me with the coldest eyes I have ever seen. "Do you know who I am?" He asked, clearly outraged that I had entered his personal space. "I'll be honest," I replied, "No."" Well, take it from me, you don't want to. Now go away, I'm busy." At that he turned his attention back to the quivering Ratfinks who had retreated to their doorways. "As for you wankers, keep away from my bitches or I'll be back." With his message delivered he turned and walked away.

I spotted 'Old Man Ratfink' and walked over to him as he stood by his front door. "Anyone want to make a formal complaint?" The door was slammed in my face. I took that as a no.

By this point everyone was doubled over in laughter.

It turns out some members of the Ratfinks had given one of 'Scouse Adams' 'working girls' a slap, temporarily reducing his financial income. Not surprisingly, no official complaints were made from either party".

Little did I know at the time but about 18 months later I would have the dubious pleasure of meeting Mr Adams and I can confirm he was every bit as large and gnarly as Tony had described him. I was tasked with visiting him in HM Prison Armley in Leeds with some follow up enquiries regarding an assault I was dealing with in which he was an alleged witness. On our arrival my colleague and I were seated in the communal visiting area while a prison warder went to fetch him. Several minutes later the biggest man I have ever seen who resembled Desperate Dan only bigger, uglier and no where near as friendly approached my table. He stopped some two or three yards short of me and the room went very quiet and noticeably darker. "I don't know these twats" he bellowed. "I've got fuck all to say" Then he immediately turned around and walked back to his cell pushing the warder out of his way. So no information there then not even a cuertasy hand shake.

"Could only happen to you," shouted Lightbulb. "Who's up next?" The drinks were flowing and the volume of laughter and chatter had raised a few levels.

"Okay I'm up," shouted Ricky. "I was working with Millsy the other Saturday night outside the 'Walkin' night club on Leeds Road. (Remember, this is the 80s licensing hours were in existence and as such, piss heads loved the weekend when night clubs offered them that much needed extra drinking time).

It was a warm night and there were people milling about all over. Mostly good banter with the occasional insult aimed at the boys in blue. Nothing unusual had occurred until we heard a massive smash coming from the direction of the night club. As I looked over I could see a car had been driven into the double doors of the club entrance and people were gathering round shouting and waving their fists. I put out a shout on my radio for back up as me and Millsy ran towards the melee.

We were only a few hundred yards away so we were there in no time. By now half a dozen bouncers were having a heated discussion with a few of the local piss heads, and sure enough the fists started flying. It turned out that earlier one of those involved had been barred entry to the club, so he had attempted to run down the offending doorman in his car. As me and Millsy tried to keep the two factions apart, some of the onlookers took offence to us spoiling their entertainment and started pulling us away. It was a fairly hopeless situation to put it mildly until all of a sudden I could hear a panting sound in my ear. As I turned to look around I saw Sgt Goody standing by my side struggling to catch his breath. "Where's the back up Sarge?" I asked him. "I'm it." he gasped. "There were no units available." For fuck sake!

Sgt Goody was the desk Sgt who I had radioed minutes earlier for back up. Obviously realising there wasn't any, he had left the control room and run the half mile from the nick to the night club to help us out. What a star! He was no spring chicken but his concern for our welfare had sparked him into action and he pitched in giving them as good as we were getting till the cavalry arrived."

Goody! Goody! Goody! Drink for Sgt Goody. So more drinks it was. Appropriately another Sgt, Sgt Wells took the next turn.

Sgt Wells was a guy in his late thirties, not overly big but as fit as a butcher's dog and not afraid to get involved.

"Okay, most of you have probably heard this one but I'm going to tell you anyway. The town centre police had been looking for a guy for the last few weeks who'd been sexually assaulting women and some of the victims had received serious injuries. Although all the attacks seemed to be confined to the town centre, his description had been passed to neighbouring divisions in an effort to bring him in.

The descriptions for the suspect were pretty accurate, detailing him as a white male 6' to 6'2'', heavy build, short black hair and scruffy. A photofit had been circulated with his description. There was an accompanying instruction not to approach this guy alone. Anyway, a couple of days ago I was making my way out of the town centre having given evidence at a court hearing. As a result, although I had my uniform on it was covered by my rain coat. I had only walked a few hundred yards when my attention was drawn to a guy walking across Manchester Road away from the bus station to my side of the road. I stopped for a moment to get a good look as he passed right in front of me. It was a Eureka moment as I immediately recognised him as the suspect from the sex attacks.

I was buzzing. This would be a great collar, especially as I wasn't on my own patch. I turned to follow the guy as he made his way up the road. He definitely looked a handy fucker and as I was now technically off duty, I had no radio to call for assistance. No problem, I thought this is a main route into town for a lot of traffic so I'll just stay close until I see a patrol car then I'll make my move.

Where's the coppers when you need 'em? I seemed to walk for ages without seeing a single cop car. Then suddenly there it was, a divisional Transit van travelling down the road towards me. This was my chance. I got as close as I could to the suspect and just before the div van reached me, I pounced, leaping onto the blokes back, I knocked him to the floor. Shit! As I wrestled on the pavement to keep hold of him, I looked up in horror as I saw the div van driving straight past me, driven by the station caretaker who had just taken the van for a wash. Realising he'd been rumbled, the suspect began to lash out throwing me from side to side in an effort to break free. Luckily for me, in the same fashion as buses, having seen one div van another one appeared, this time loaded with coppers. Seeing the commotion they pulled up and suffice to say the guy was nicked".

By now the room was rocking with heavily intoxicated, off duty coppers.

"That's your lot guys and girls. I'm knackered and we are out of beer". Came a shout from the barman. "Make your way to your dwellings and I will stock up and we can go again tomorrow".

23

One For My Baby

This one came early in my service, It occurred while still on my probation period being trained by my tutor constable PC Andy Waters. It was the early hours of the morning, I was in the passenger seat as Andy drove the marked patrol car around the streets of Laisterdyke. I was reflecting how this period of the day was generally fairly quiet when we received a radio call to attend Beach Street following a report of a possible house break-in taking place. The caller had been anonymous and didn't give a house number, chances were it was nothing more than a noisy party but we made our way to the area to take a look. As we turned onto the street the lack of a house number instantly became more of a problem than we had bargained for. The street was a good quarter of a mile long and was pitch black. Andy turned off the car headlights so as not to give our presence away as we slowly edged up the street, both viewing opposite sides of the road looking for anything out of place. As it turned out we didn't have to look to hard after all because about two thirds of the way up the hill Andy brought the car to a halt and turned the engine off. We had stopped outside the front of a two storey terraced house. There was no doubting this was the place as the front room lights illuminated the front yard through a hugh hole in the six feet square living room window. The instant we left the car and started walking towards the front of the house I could hear a male voice emanating from the building through the broken window. It wasn't exactly shouting but there were definitely threatening tones. As I peered into the living room through what remained of the window the sight that greeted me was not at all what I had anticipated. Facing towards me at the far side of the room a guy in his early 30's was slumped on the floor with his back pressed against the wall his legs stretched out in front of him. Bizzarley he wasn't wearing a stitch of clothing, but was covered from head to toe in blood. A second bloke in his late twenties, who had his back to me was leaning over the first guy and firing questions at him. "Do you want some more of that you wanker? Hey I'm asking you, do you want some more? I can't hear you. Okay I'll give you a bit more." The guy on the floor was mumbling apparently unable to speak. Could have been that he was drunk, on drugs or he had taken one to many blows to the head maybe a combination of all three. In any event his opportunity to reply was cut short as another smashing right hand crashed into the side of his face jolting his head in the opposite direction. "Oy. Pack it in police." Andy and I shouted in unison. The guy on the floor remained expressionless and seemed oblivious to our presence. The aggressor who was built like a heavy weight boxer and wore a white tee shirt which had turned a light shade of pink due to his oppos blood, turned to face us in a relatively calm and controlled manner. "Okay guys no problem I'm pretty much done here." He offered in a matter of fact way. "Glad to hear it. Get that front door open lets get this sorted out." I instructed him. Just like that he turned and made his way from the living room out into the hallway.

Alongside Andy I stood by the front door and listened as the hit man fumbled with the lock on the inside. After a couple of minutes the noise stopped and seconds later a voice bellowed out from the direction of the broken window. "Sorry guys. I can't get it open. I'm just going to give that twat a bit more."

Shit now what. The window sill was at head height and large jagged fragments of glass filled the edges of the window frame. A quick bit of DIY with my truncheon cleared away most of the broken glass from the lower edge of the frame. I turned towards Andy who was leaning forward with his hands cupped by his knees, gesturing for me to use his hands as a leg up and in through the window. "Wait up. How come I'm the one going in?" I enquired. "Cos' you're the newbie. Get in." Came the none negotiable reply.

Now I'm no big fan of health and safety which back then wasn't a problem. There wasn't any! That said, right at that moment I had to confess I was having one or two welfare concerns as I was pushed through the jagged opening. Minor things really, like severing a main artery on the shards of glass or taking a kick to the head from my mate in the pink top. As it turned out my fears were unfounded. Much to my surprise, and relief, as I scrambled through the pile of broken glass the big lad reached over and helped me to my feet before turning away and placing his hands on the back of his head. "Sorry I've caused you so much trouble." He said quietly. "I've done what I had to do. I'm ready to go now." I handcuffed him and walked him to the front door where I let in Andy and two other coppers who had responded to our call for back up. I directed the back up lads to the injured guy who was still sat on the living room floor looking dazed and battered, they tended to him until the ambulance arrived a couple of minutes later.

As for me and Andy we took the big lad to the bridewell where his clothes were seized for evidence in exchange for a one size fits all boiler suit.

Prior to commencing our interview with the prisoner we received information from the officers at the scene. It turned out that having removed the big lad from the house, his semi-naked wife had made her way into the living room, having been hiding in an upstairs bedroom, and threw her arms around her blood soaked lover. Details which gave us a clearer picture as to why this assault had taken place.

Sure enough during the subsequent interview the big lad explained that for some time he had suspected that his wife was having an affair with his best friend, who I think its fair to say was now his ex best mate. He continued that after a lengthy drinking session he had gone to his friends house and let himself in through the front room window, with the aid of a brick. Having entered the house his worst fears had been confirmed when he discovered both his wife and his best friend naked together in the upstairs bedroom. He explained that he snapped and dragged his 'friend' down the stairs where he dished out some summary justice. Though many people, myself included could see why this guy had taken the action he did, unfortunately his views on justice didn't fit with the laws of the land and he was subsequently handed a suspended prison sentence at crown court.

His ex friends injuries amounted to a night in hospital with concussion, several stitches to a number of cuts and bruising.

24

Home Alone

Night shifts were always approached with more anticipation than any of the other shifts for obvious reasons. Whilst crimes of any type can occur at any time, statistically the majority of serious crimes, violent assaults, burglaries, car thefts etc occur during the night time hours. No coincidence that these hours are also when the highest volume of alcohol is consumed.

I think its fair to say most coppers entered the night shifts with similar feelings but leaving a wife and two tots in my family home whilst working across the other side of the City added an extra twist.

Those concerns became very real one night while I was riding shotgun alongside Pc Burrows.

Mike Burrows stood 6' 6'' tall and was the original gentle giant, unless anyone crossed him of course. Mike was a qualified quick response driver and was waiting for a vacancy on the motorway patrol unit to further his chosen career path.

It was about 2.30 in the morning when a message came over the police radio specifically directed at me. "Tim don't be alarmed but Jan (My wife) has just rung Toller lane nick (the sub-divisional police station which covered my house) reporting that one or more people are trying the back door handle on your house.

Don't panic, I was terrified a feeling of helplessness like never before, my house backed onto parkland with practically no over-looking houses, it had never occurred to me before just how vulnerable my wife and my 4 year old and 12 month old sons were. Although I was only four or five miles from my home right at that moment it felt like I was a million miles away. Ruth my control room operative continued "Toller Lane units are on route as we speak and their controller is keeping Jan on the phone." As Ruth's words were sinking in I turned to Mike and without a word being uttered we were on our way to my family home. There was no doubt that Mike's advanced driving skills were are bonus right at that moment but that said we were hampered by the lack of performance from the high mileage bog standard Ford Escort patrol car.

The radio went again. It was Ruth. "Tim I've managed to get a live link with Toller Lane, you will be able to hear Jan talking to their controller." The next voice I heard was the female voice of their control op. "You'll be fine Jan I have a number of units on their way to you, they'll be there in no time." Then Jans voice. I don't know what was going through my head at this point but hearing her voice came as a massive relief. "I'm okay. I'm sorry to bother everyone. I'm just scared with my young boys in the house and Tim being at work." "Don't you worry Jan. The units are nearly with you, and Tims aware of what's happening and he's making his way to you now."

As Mike pushed the old Escort for all it was worth we sped through the town centre and along Thornton Road our destination now less than 2 miles away.

Then for a split second the world stood still as Jans voice flooded from the radio. The fear in her voice was palpable. "There's someone running down the drive at the side of the house towards the back door." Then silence for what felt like an eternity, but which in reality was a the briefest moment, before the Toller Lane controller announced "Its okay Jan. You're safe. Look out of the front window the units are there."

Just minutes later and I was home. Four patrol cars and a rapid response vehicle filled the turning circle at the end of the cul-de-sac. I checked that Jan was okay and gave her a bear hug before thanking the Toller Lane lads. They pointed out two young blokes sitting in the back of one of the patrol cars, and explained to me how they were well known local villains. It turned out that having broken into my car parked on the driveway these two low lifes, both high on drink and drugs had then attempted to jemmy open the back door of the house. Having heard the police units arriving they had hidden behind a shed at the foot of my garden, before being found and arrested for attempted burglary.

I thanked the lads again as I reflected on the barrage of emotions which had pounded my head in the space of those last fifteen minutes.

Off Duty

Before I move on its worth mentioning another notable incident which took place in my back garden some twelve months later. Though not strictly a police matter, it did involve the use of my police issue handcuffs. No nothing like that, but read on I think you'll find this one interesting, maybe a little disturbing.

I take great pride in introducing my dad Bert at this point, as without him its unlikely the subject of this story would ever have entered my life, though

I'm not sure that's something I would thank him for. At the time Bert was in his early fifties, around 5' 8" tall, though he would do his utmost to convince people he was nearer 5' 10" tall. He was a stocky fella with the strength of an ox, old school hard as nails, afraid of no one, but with a real soft centre.

My old man ran a rehabilitation hostel for ex-offenders a little more than a mile from my house. This had been my family home for the majority of my teenage years and when I first joined the police force it was often joked amongst the inmates that as fast as I locked em up Bert would rehabilitate them and get them back on the street. My dad was fully committed to his extended family and would go well beyond the call of duty to give anyone a second chance provided the individual had the same commitment. This confidence and faith in his house mates could on occasion be slightly misguided but never more so than with one particular inmate. Ron Mason.

Mason was in his mid twenties a similar height and build to my old man. He had neat, short cut fair hair and was generally well dressed and polite. Though he had no serious convictions he had been abandoned by his parents as a baby and had anger management issues and was known to have previously used drugs. That said there was nothing in his past which could have forewarned anyone of the extent of his darker side.

There was an unwritten rule between me and dad which was that my home address would always remain private from the inmates, in the event that someone may feel they had an axe to grind with the law.

Like so many rules this one was broken one night when Bert came to my house to drop something off. In the back of his car at the time was Mason. In truth I don't think anyone really registered at the time that the cardinal rule had been breached. This lack of awareness would come back to haunt us some two or three months later.

I was getting changed in my bedroom early one evening when Jan shouted up to me that we had a visitor. I wasn't expecting company and something in Jan's voice suggested that this wasn't a particularly welcome caller, so quickly made my way downstairs. The sight that greeted me as I entered the living room was Mason sat on my sofa alongside the family pet labrador Bobby. Initially Mason seemed unaware that I had entered the room and continued to hold the dog with less of a cuddle more of a bear hug. Bobby looked at me with wide eyes that pleaded "Get this mad man off me. Quick!" Something was definitely not right, Mason had taken Bobby for a walk dozens of times in the past whenever I visited my dad and they genuinely seemed to like each other. This didn't feel right Mason seemed oblivious to what he was doing and Bobby was clearly distressed by this crazy man who was currently expelling the air from his lungs. "You alright Mason?" I enquired, dreading the answer. Mason seemed startled as he turned to face me. "Errr nooo. I dooon't feeel sooo goood." He replied in a slow drawn out eerie, monotone voice. His pupils were wide and his eyes were working independently from each other. In an instant my worst fears were realised, Mason was off his head on drugs. Bobby was starting to panic now as Mason seemed to be gripping him even tighter. "Iiii looove yooou Bobbeeey yooorrre myyy bessst fieeend. Nooo ooone elssse underrstandsss meee." "Okay Mason lets get some fresh air pal." I had dealt with a good number of drug addicts at best they are unpredictable and more often than not aggressive. I had no idea what he had taken but he was as high as anyone I had ever encountered. I had to get him away from the dog and out of the house as quickly as I could. "Come on pal you're scaring Bobby. Lets sit outside for a while." "Nooo I looove Bobbeeey." "Yeah I know you do but he's shaking, let him go now." It was like walking on egg shells, if he was going to kick off I wanted him outside away from my family. Mason still wasn't for moving so I had to wrestle his arms from around my dog. As I lifted Mason to his feet and began to usher him towards the kitchen. I told Jan to take the dog upstairs and stay there with our two sons who were blissfully unaware of what was occurring. As Jan disappeared with Bobby up the stairs I took hold of Mason's arm and guided him through the kitchen and and sat him on the back step where I sat alongside him. He was talking relentlessly most of which was incoherent and devoid of any sense. I was trying to establish where he had been and what he had taken when Jan appeared behind me and asked, "Is there anything I can do?" "Yeah" I answered. "Go ring my dad tell him what's going on and ask him to drive down so we can get Mason home." The very mention of my old man sparked an unexpected reaction from Mason who stood up demanding, "Dooon't telll Berrrt. Dooon't telll Berrrt." In the same drawn out robotic voice as before, only this time with a heightened sense of agitation. Jan shot back into the house to make the call while I attempted to reassure Mason that everything was fine. I had no sooner succeeded in getting him reseated when Jan reappeared. "I spoke with your dad he's in the middle of watching a film. He said he'll come round when its finished." At this news me and Mason both leapt to our feet, and he set off walking around and around the garden repeating the words "Dooon't telll Berrrt, dooon't telll Berrrt." I looked straight at Jan and spurted out. "Ring him again and tell him to get here NOW!!" Time was not on my side, the junkie was working himself into a frenzy and was likely to blow at any moment. Jan dashed back into the house to make a second call conveying to my dad the growing urgency of the situation. I remained by the back door focused on the bubbling volcano that was Mason. Moments later Jan reappeared to let me know my dad was on his way. Nothing I could do now but wait. It felt like forever, but ten minutes or so later I heard I heard a car pull up at the front of the house. I was anticipating an intense explosion and I wasn't disappointed. As Bert appeared at the end of the driveway Mason took one look at him and made a be line for me shouting "Yooou tooold Berrrt, yooou tooold Berrrt." His charge for me was interrupted by my dad who crashed into him chest to chest clamping his arms around Mason's shoulders in the collision. I saw my chance and made a short dash forwards before executing a rugby style tackle around Mason's legs, taking him to the ground with my old man smashing down on top of him. Though Mason was a fit, strong lad this impact should have been enough to subdue men twice his size, but whatever he consumed that day was playing its part and he was thrashing around like a man possessed. Despite the best efforts of both me and Bert it was proving a struggle to keep him pinned down. I shouted out to Jan to fetch my handcuffs and minutes later she threw the cuffs towards me. Now all I had to do was to get them onto this crazy guy. I've no idea how long it took for us to get Mason's arms around his back and get the cuffs in place, but it took every ounce of bloody energy I know that. Once we had secured his arms we dragged him kicking and screaming to the back of Bert's car. We forced him onto the back seat and I joined him sitting directly behind the drivers seat incase Mason got the urge to lurch forward and smash into back of my dad while he was driving.

This seating arrangement had become second nature to me having been shown a series of pictures at training school depicting an arrest which had gone badly wrong. They related to two coppers who had nicked a drunk and failed to search him before he was placed on the back seat of their patrol car after which they both climbed into the front seats. As the officers transported their prisoner to the cells he leant forward and using a stanley knife which he had hidden inside his jacket he slashed the drivers throat and inflicted several serious cuts to the passengers face, before escaping on foot. Miraculously both the officers survived. For me it was a warning message I wasn't going to forget.

As for the current predicament, Mason, Bert had chosen to keep the incident in-house believing it was nothing more than a blip which he could deal with in the morning. Not knowing at that time that the evenings fun and games weren't over just yet.

It was as we started our short trip that Mason went into some type of trance. The same guy who moments earlier had been a violent thrashing machine was now sat along side me gently rocking backwards and forwards, his gaze was fixed as he quietly chanted in some unrecognisable language. Give me back the fighter this was terrifying, like witnessing a demonic possession. His unnerving behaviour continued for the remainder of the journey until we pulled up alongside the open up and over door to my dads garage. Surprisingly Mason remained in his strange self contained state as me and Bert eased him from the back of the car and stood him inside the empty garage. "Okay, lets get the cuffs off and get him inside." Suggested Bert. "Not sure that's a good idea. Lets get him inside first." I responded without hesitation. "No come on. He's calmed down now he'll be fine." Insisted my dad. "You've got to trust me." I repeated "Get him inside first." Bert was having none of it. "Get the cuffs off. I want to get him bedded down so he can sleep it off." "Your call." I conceded, realising my old man wasn't for budging. There are times when you'd rather you weren't right and this was one of them. As soon as I released Mason's wrists the monster erupted. This time we faced an additional hazard in the form of a metal handcuff attached to the end of his flailing right arm. "Shit ! Here we go again." In a repeat of the move we had performed earlier, I took a grip round his legs while Bert grappled him around the chest forcing him to the ground. Deja vu. Just as before we had Mason grounded but moving him anywhere would be a different problem. Out of the blue a timid voice broke my thoughts. "Do you need any help there." Before I could think of a sarcastic response my dad shouted. "Grab his legs" "No, no, not mine Rodney. Get hold of Masons legs." I quickly clarified.

Now I'm not going to be hard on Rodney, another of the hostel inmates, because he was a fraudster not a fighter, in his early sixties and built like a whiff of wind. But at least he was there and pitching in.

What happened next had to be seen to be fully appreciated. The plan was for Rodney to take hold of Mason's ankles freeing me up to get the handcuffs back in place. In fact what happened was the instant I released my grip Mason began kicking out wildly. Rodney was immediately reduced to clinging onto one leg, and cling on he did. Whether it was fear or shear determination Rodney was not letting go of his designated limb. As Mason kicked out to the right so Rodders followed, sailing through the air, only to be snapped back as Mason's leg lashed back towards the direction from which it had just travelled. So the pattern continued Rodney clinging to Mason's leg for all he was worth, grimacing and screaming with each change of direction, as he flew backwards and forwards through the air like a demented trapeze act. As mesmerising as this flying display was, the problem remained. We weren't getting anywhere. Heavy duty reinforcements were required and I new just where to find them. I left the garage melee and ran into the hostel and up the stairs to the first floor and in through the first bedroom door, flicking on the lights as I entered. "What the fuck. What's going on?" Thundered Tony from beneath his bed sheets. "It's okay pal its me. Mason's kicking off in the garage, we could use some help." Tony's large bearded head emerged from beneath the covers. "Let me get some pants on. I'll be right there."

Tony was in his mid forties, not much over 5' 9" tall and generally resembled a silver back gorilla with the strength to match. He had been in and out of nick for the best part of his life generally for alcohol fuelled fighting. That said he was a good ally to have especially in a tight spot.

I left Tony to get dressed and dashed back to the garage. Not much had changed Mason was still pinned to the concrete floor by my old man and Rodney was perfecting his flying skills. "Take a break pal, you've done a great job Rodney." I assured him as I gathered in Mason's legs. Rodney looked relieved as he slumped to the floor exhausted, just in time to see Tony appear through the side door. "Need some help there Bert?" He bellowed, as he launched his full body weight onto the small of Mason's back who let out a blood curdling scream before collapsing motionless. His fight was over as he lay there motionless the air drained from his lungs. The four of us carried the groaning Mason unceremoniously up to Tony's bedroom where he remained to sleep off his cocktail of drink and drugs, with Tony volunteering as night watchman.

Although that brought the evenings activities to a close, what occurred a few months later sent shivers down my spine when the full extent of Mason's capabilities were exposed.

Following a night out on the town, a middle aged school teacher was walking home with a couple of his friends oblivious to what was about to happen. Unfortunately for him also out that evening was Mason who was laying in wait behind a tall stone wall. As the unsuspecting teacher turned the corner Mason leapt forward and brought a concrete paving slab crashing down on the mans head crushing his skull and killing him instantly.

No reason or motive for this senseless murder was ever established.

Mason himself calmly handed himself into the police and was subsequently sentenced to a life behind bars.

25

CID

Criminal Investigation Department

Some nine years into my career I had finally realised my dream, or so I thought! My desire to become a detective and take down the bad guys would, in reality, prove to be more a nightmare.

Training School

Training school was based in Wakefield, a six week residential course. It was divided almost equally between the study of head mashing, lengthy, crime definitions, and countless lectures.

The definitions which had to be learned parrot fashion covered offences such as:

Burglary

A person is guilty of burglary if he enters a building or a part of a building as a trespasser with intent to commit any of the following,

Theft

Grievous bodily harm

Unlawful damage

And so it went on, learn the full definitions for theft, GBH, criminal damage. Plus the explanations for what constitutes a building, what is intention, etc, etc. And that was just one law!

Along with the intense studying, there were endless lectures, which came in many forms. Interview techniques, report writing skills, court etiquette, forensics, surveillance techniques and fraud investigation. Without question the most interesting lectures were delivered by renowned pathologists, who's intelligence and wit accompanied by explicit slide shows of murder scenes, left lasting impressions.

The remainder of the course was spent on the piss drinking the pubs and clubs of Wakefield dry.

The classroom studies and lectures were interspersed by weekly exams all of which had to be passed to progress further on the course, which concluded after six weeks with a brutal final exam. The exam results were combined with the assessments from the course lecturers to give an overall mark.

I passed. I wasn't in the top group but I had achieved my goal.

Laisterdyke police Station

Back at my sub division I returned to uniform duties while I waited for a vacancy to come up in within the CID.

I waited and I waited. Many of the lads from my course who I had kept in touch with had already been placed mostly within a week or two. I waited three months.

Still my day finally came and I was looking forward to a new chapter, albeit this was only a probationary post.

In truth what set off slowly would eventually grind to a halt.

On reflection it could be there is an element of luck with regard to the team you are attached to. Mine consisted of DCI Burns, DS Holmes and DC Irons. These were all decent blokes and bloody good detectives, but I soon realised that drinking played a big part in the life of an 80's detective, in this team at least.

The first thing I noticed was the volume of paper work. Huge numbers crime reports were passed over to the CID from the uniform section, serious assaults, burglaries, robberies, car thefts effectively all the big cases. Each of these needed to be followed up with visits to the crime scene, witness interviews and statements, forensic reports, suspect arrests and processing and finally compiling court files.

Keeping on top of the paper work was never one of my strengths as a uniform cop and I quickly started to feel out of my depth. Try as I may my in tray never seemed to go down.

In the main for the majority of my shifts I would accompany my team members attending crime scenes or sitting in on interviews that is until something juicy came along then I would be assigned to the office to answer the phone.

There were the odd moments that broke this pattern, such as one evening when DS Holmes' drinking was interrupted by a report of a suspicious death. When I attended the address with him it transpired that a known criminal had hung himself from his loft. On entering the house and reaching the top of the stairs, a lifeless body with a thick rope around his neck was laid out on the landing. Paramedics had cut the body down in an effort to resuscitate the body ... without success. DS Holmes' response was, "No worries if he's definitely dead. There's not a lot more we can do now." He then instructed the uniformed officer who had been first on the scene to write up the details and let him have a copy of the report. After which we returned to the boozer.

Another time I was sent to an isolated farm house to sit with the occupants who had received a phone call that a man was going to visit them with a shotgun to conclude an ongoing feud. Of course, I was unarmed and was told not to do anything stupid, just contact the station some twenty minutes drive away, when the guy showed up. He never did.

Following an allegation of repeated anal sex by her ex-partner from the landlady of a local hostelry, my babysitting skills were called on again. The 'victim' had heard on the grapevine that her ex was planning to return to her pub after the dinner time session was finished (remember, licensing hours in the 80s), when he intended to repeat his previous sexual assaults. The rest of my team obviously saw this as a great opportunity to obtain a few free beers following which they departed and I was left to arrest the assailant should he return. He never did.

I don't know if it was just my over-active mind but there seemed to be a pattern forming here. I seemed to be getting a lot of jobs that came to nothing but kept me out of the loop for a few hours.

On another occasion I was assigned to accompany one of the fraud squad officers whilst he investigated an embezzlement case which ran into hundreds of thousands of pounds. Now finally it looked like I was getting involved in something a bit juicy. But no. The reality was the opposite. Me at the side of the fraud officer for 8 hours whilst he poured over endless reams of paper containing more numbers than I'd ever seen in my life. The detective himself was a nice enough fella and he tried to explain what he was doing but unless you had a degree in maths, it wasn't going to make good listening.

One afternoon we had a genuine enquiry to make at a pub and together with DC Irons, we attended the salubrious Farmer's Arms. The landlord wished to report an internal theft which he believed one of his staff may have been involved in and he greeted us at the rear door of the premises. He welcomed us inside and ushered us upstairs to his living area. The problem occurred as the landlord and DC Irons disappeared from view at the top of the stairs. I encountered a second welcoming party in the form of two huge Dobermann Pinschers. Now, I am a dog guy. I love dogs. I've always owned a dog but I'm more your Labrador kind of bloke. Whilst I was weighing up my options, one of the dogs decided to introduce himself and not in a subtle way, I might add. No, not subtle. He charged at me and head butted me right in the crown jewels. Not satisfied with the pain he had already inflicted, he now commenced to push his head into my groin, pinning me against the wall for all he was worth. His message had been received loud and clear and with tears welling in my eyes from he initial impact, the head, full of teeth, buried in my crutch decided to add some sound effects in the form of a deep constant snarl. I was fucked. I couldn't move and I was afraid to call for help in case my manhood was ripped from my pants. I remained at the dog's mercy for a good ten minutes until the two men appeared at the foot of the stairs. DC Irons took one look at my predicament and commenced to laugh uncontrollably. A snap of the fingers from the landlord and the two dogs backed down and disappeared through an open door.

To rub salt into the wound, no report was made as the items originally thought to be missing had magically reappeared. And so my CID initiation continued until one afternoon when I was involved in a case that both angered and saddened me in equal measures.

It involved a family living in a council housing estate, which social services had been monitoring for several weeks following information they had received from staff at a local junior school regarding one of their pupils.

The family consisted of husband and wife Mr and Mrs X and their three girls, Kim 15, Joe 13 and Miranda 7. Mr X was a large barrel chested scruffy individual with dark unkempt hair and a stubbly beard, in his mid thirties. Essentially a drunkard and a bully who had never worked a day in his life. Mrs X was also in her mid thirties short and thin with a gaunt face. The two younger girls both appeared under nourished and withdrawn, while the older girl Kim was slightly plump and very more outspoken.

The school had expressed their concerns regarding the timid and reclusive nature of Miranda who, on occasion, had displayed bruising to her wrists. More recently she had wet herself several times during class. The two female child care officers assigned the case had previously made a number of visits to the family home and with each visit had become increasingly concerned with regard to the living conditions and the children's welfare. During their most recent visit the two officers had been ushered into the house by Kim due to her parents being intoxicated. Once inside the house they had met with a barrage of threats and verbal abuse from both Mr and Mrs X. At this time the social workers had retreated from the house to implement a care order for the children.

Now I don't pretend to know the full procedure to activate such a plan but it seems it takes a considerable amount of report writing and meetings with the powers that be to cut through the red tape in order for it to be sanctioned.

However once the necessary paper work was in place a date was set and action plan formulated.

All the indicators in this case lead us to believe that the young girls may have been subjected to some form of sexual assault and accordingly two specially trained police women, together with the women from social services were appointed to head the team. They were backed up by, DCI Burns, (the hierarchy liked to get involved with the higher profile cases), DS Holmes, DC Irons and myself, we in turn were accompanied by four uniform coppers, essentially to cover exit points from the house and deal with any public order incidents.

It would be reasonable to think this added up to a touch of over kill, but where children were involved risks had to be minimised.

The day arrived and off we went in our little convoy.

On our arrival at the address a couple of the uniformed lads were posted by the rear of the house whilst the detectives accompanied the four female members of the team to the front door. The door was partially open and after receiving no answer to repeated knocking with a feather, we entered the house on mass.

The front room was exactly as it had been described. A shit tip. There were numerous empty beer cans and whiskey bottles strewn across the carpet. Overflowing ashtrays were dotted everywhere. The smell was overwhelming, a combination of stale cigarette smoke, alcohol, urine and body odour.

Mr X, wearing only a pair of shorts was slumped into one of a pair of thread bare, brown corduroy armchairs, both of which were riddled with cigarette burns and tears. On his knee was the youngest girl Miranda, she was naked.

The other children Joe and Kim occupied the second chair wearing only knickers and dirty tee shirts.

Mrs X was just entering the living room wearing a pair of tatty jeans and a black bra, from the kitchen at the rear of the house.

Bizarrely none of the occupants seemed concerned at their shortage of clothing, the state of the house or more importantly the fact that several police officers and social workers had entered the room. That was until the lead social worker announced to Mr and Mrs X that we were taking the children into care. Without moving from his chair Mr X made his feelings clear. "You can all go fuck yourselves. Nobodies taking my kids." Mrs X remained silent, clearly terrified, not of losing her children but of upsetting her slob of a husband. The two younger girls also remained silent and motionless, again most likely through fear of retribution from their father. In contrast the oldest girl, Kim was having none of it. She launched herself forward from her chair towards the two social workers. "You can't take us from me dad. He loves us. What will he do without us ?"She screamed at the top of her voice. Tears streaming down her face. Kim was prevented from reaching her target by one of the police women, but those words would haunt us all. She was so psychologically damaged and brain washed that she believed what her father did to her was normal. Mayhem followed as Mr X leapt to his feet casting Miranda to the floor as he attempted to make it across the room to Kim. That was never going to happen and I launched my shoulder into his chest knocking him to the floor, landing on top of him and pinning him to the ground. I was quickly assisted by a couple of my colleagues and X was going nowhere. The room was full of noise, screaming, shouting and crying as I dragged Mr X to his feet and handcuffed him. I remembered wondering how his face had acquired a number of injuries in the short space of time from him hitting the floor to being stood back on his feet. I never did find out. Across the room I could see the two social workers trying to wrestle the two younger girls away from their mother.

It was a difficult situation to absorb, almost surreal, a family being pulled apart. The young girls terrified at being taken from the only life they had ever known.

A life they had been conditioned not to question, but to accept as normal.

As the parents were ushered from the house in cuffs, and the girls were taken into care by the social services, myself and the other detectives began our search of the house. The filth and stench was reason enough for the premises not to be suitable for young children, and that was before we uncovered evidence which shocked even the more seasoned coppers. Pornographic polaroid photographs showing the girls in various sexual acts. Pornographic video tapes. All manor of sexual lingerie which included masks. A large number of adult toys. In the main none of these items were hidden but seemed to be easily accessible from draws and cupboards, throughout most of the house. The most disturbing items recovered were a variety of restraints which would subsequently be identified in a number of the photographs already seized.

Yet again I was to play no further part in this investigation, though on this occasion I cant say I was disappointed. I'd seen enough.

Just one week later I was back in uniform on the pretext there were no vacancies forthcoming.

Initially I took this as a failure to make the grade but on reflection my lack of beer drinking skills probably didn't help. Still whatever the reason I returned to doing what I did best. Plodding the streets.

26

The writing on the wall

Not long after my return to uniform duties I was forced off work for 6 weeks with a burst eardrum. It was an disguised warning that my time on the job was limited. On my return to work there had been numerous personnel changes and a new policing protocol seemed to have swept in over night. Just like that it was as though I didn't belong, I felt out of sink, like a fish out of water.

I convinced myself everything would sort itself out and I continued going through the motions for several more months.

But without realising it, things weren't getting any better they were getting worse, a lot worse. I wasn't sleeping, I couldn't concentrate on even the simplest tasks, I was drinking more, and I wasn't doing my uniform justice.

In truth I was oblivious, I new something wasn't right but I wasn't aware how serious things had become. The stress from all the shit I had seen and dealt with over the past 10 years had finally taken its toll, and mentally I was burnt out.

The end finally came one night when just prior to commencing an undercover operation I reached for the phone and rang my wife. I recall the conversation.

"I can't do this anymore."

"What do you mean."

"I don't want to be here."

"Come home then."

And just like that it was all over.

How many partners would do that ? Be that understanding !

Not many I know that.

My wife almost certainly saved what was left of my sanity.

I didn't know at the time what a mess my head was in, but after several weeks on sick leave, during which time I effectively locked myself away I was diagnosed and medically retired from the force with a mental, or nervous breakdown, a condition which in the modern era would probably be labelled PTSD (Post Traumatic Stress Disorder). It would take many years before I could accept just how ill I had become and many more before I was able to regain a degree of control over my life.

Maybe that's a journey to share another time.

Acknowledgements

Thank you to my loving wife and best friend Jan for standing by me during the toughest times in my life and career, and for her constant encouragement, unwavering patience and constructive criticism whilst compiling the pages for my book.

My editors

Jenny Mills my lovely daughter in law.

Philip Mills my baby brother.

Deborah Robinson my other best friend and typist.

Last, but by no means least, many thanks to my two sons Dave and Roo for always being there when I need them, and for enduring my stories over and over again. You are largely responsible for giving me the confidence to turn my memories into written words.

Thank you all xx

Disclaimer

This is a work of creative nonfiction. The events are portrayed to the best of my memory. While all the stories in this book are true, some names and identifying details have been changed to protect the privacy of the people involved.

Printed in Great Britain
by Amazon